Christopher Columbus

The authentic Letters of Columbus

Christopher Columbus

The authentic Letters of Columbus

ISBN/EAN: 9783743324329

Manufactured in Europe, USA, Canada, Australia, Japa

Cover: Foto ©ninafisch / pixelio.de

Manufactured and distributed by brebook publishing software (www.brebook.com)

Christopher Columbus

The authentic Letters of Columbus

INDEX TO CONTENTS.

		PAGE
History and general description of the letters of Columbus		99
Translations		118
I.	Letter to Ferdinand and Isabella, between July 5th and September 25th, 1493.	118
II.	Letter to Ferdinand and Isabella concerning supplies for and the government of the Indes, without date, but probably written before the second voyage	121
III.	Letter to Ferdinand and Isabella from Granada, February 6th, 1502	123
IV.	Letter to Nicolo Oderigo from Seville, March 21st, 1502	127
V.	Letter to the Governors of the Bank of St. George, Genoa, from Seville, April 2nd, 1502	129
VI.	Letter to Father Gaspar Corricio (a Carthusian monk at the monastery of Las Cuevas), San Lucar, April 4th, 1502.	131
VII.	Letter to Father Gaspar, Seville, May, 1502	133
VIII.	Letter to Father Gaspar, from Jamaica, July 7th, 1503	135
IX.	Draft upon Francisco de Morillo, Treasurer of the Crown, September 7th, 1504	137
X.	Draft upon Francisco de Morillo, September 8th, 1504	137
XI.	Draft upon Francisco de Morillo, September 9th, 1504	137
XII.	Letter to his son Diego, from Seville, November 21st, 1504	138
XIII.	Letter to his son Diego, from Seville, November 29th, 1504	143
XIV.	Letter to his son Diego, from Seville, December 1st, 1504	145
XV.	Letter to his son Diego, December 3rd, 1504	149
XVI.	Memorandum enclosed in letter to his son Diego, December 3rd, 1504	151
XVII.	Letter to his son Diego, December 13th, 1504	155
XVIII.	Letter to his son Diego from Seville, December 21st, 1504.	157

	Postscript to this letter	159
XIX.	Letter to Nicolo Oderigo, Genoese Ambassador to Spain, from Seville, December 27th, 1504	161
XX.	Letter to his son Diego, from Seville, December 29th, 1504	163
XXI.	Letter to Father Gaspar, January 4th, 1505	167
XXII.	Letter to his son Diego, January 18th, 1505	168
XXIII.	Letter to his son Diego, from Seville, February 5th, 1505	171
XXIV.	Letter to his son Diego, from Seville, February 25th, 1505	172
XXV.	Draft of letter relating to his claims against the Crown of Spain based upon the contract with the Spanish Sovereigns	173
XXVI.	Autographic statement by Columbus of gold brought from America and sold by him in Castile, date probably 1493	177
XXVII.	Original Draft by Columbus for one hundred gold castellanos, dated at Granada, October 22nd, 1501.	179
XXVIII.	Contract between Columbus and the Sovereigns— First voyage	178
XXIX.	Royal letters patent from the Sovereigns of Spain commanding the inhabitants of Palos to furnish equipment for the Columbus caravels, 1492	184
XXX.	Royal letters patent from the Sovereigns of Spain granting license to the persons accompanying Columbus on his first voyage	186
XXXI.	Letter to Louis Santangel giving an account of the first voyage and the discovery of the New World.	188
XXXII.	The will of Columbus	193

ILLUSTRATIONS.

	PAGE
Facsimile of autographic statement of gold brought from America .... Frontispiece.	
Facsimile of letter to Nicolo Oderigo, March 21st, 1502	126
Facsimile of letter to the Governors of the Bank of St. George, at Genoa, April 2nd, 1502	128
Facsimile of letter to Father Gaspar de Las Cuevas, April 4th, 1502	130
Facsimile of letter to Father Gaspar de Las Cuevas, September 4th, 1502	132
Facsimile of letter to Father Gaspar de Las Cuevas, July 7th, 1503	134
Facsimile of three letters to Francisco de Morillo, Treasurer of the Crown	136
Facsimile of portion of letter to Don Diego Columbus, November 21st, 1504	140
Facsimile of portion of letter to Don Diego Columbus, November 29th, 1504	142
Facsimile of portion of letter to Don Diego Columbus, December 1st, 1504	144
Facsimile of letter to Don Diego Columbus, December 3rd, 1504	148
Facsimile of memorandum written to Don Diego Columbus, December 3rd, 1504 . ... 150 and	152
Facsimile of portion of letter to Don Diego Columbus, December 13th, 1504	154
Facsimile of portion of letter to Don Diego Columbus, from Seville, December 21st, 1504	158
Facsimile of portion of letter to Nicolo Oderigo, December 27th, 1504	160
Facsimile of portion of letter to Don Diego Columbus, December 29th, 1504	164
Facsimile of portion of letter to Father Gaspar, January 4th, 1505	166
Facsimile of portion of letter to Don Diego Columbus, February 5th, 1505	170

The original Columbus documents described herein were exhibited under authority of the United States Government at the World's Columbian Exposition. While in charge of the Department of State at Washington, photographs were taken of the entire collection, the negatives thereby secured being subsequently presented to the Field Columbian Museum by Act of Congress. The facsimiles thus obtained, now form a part of the material in the Department of Columbus Memorial of this Institution, and it was from these photographs that the halftone illustrations in this bulletin were made.

The Authentic Letters of Columbus.

There are known to be in existence twenty-nine autographs of Christopher Columbus, not including voluminous marginal notes in his handwriting upon the pages of several books that he owned or read.

Of these autographs nineteen are letters entirely in his own hand and over his mysterious signature. Ten of them are addressed to his son Diego; four to Father Gaspar Corricio, a Carthusian monk who befriended him in his last days; two to Nicolo Oderigo, the Genoese Ambassador to Spain; two to Ferdinand and Isabella, and one to the Governors of the Bank of St. George, Genoa.

There are also six memoranda written wholly in his hand but unsigned. Two are for the information and guidance of his son Diego; two relate to his claims against the crown of Spain; one refers to his arrest and imprisonment, and the other is a statement of the disposition of the gold he brought from the Indies when he returned from his first voyage.

There are also in existence three drafts or orders for money in his handwriting, and bearing his signature; two of them addressed to Francisco de Morillo, in payment for naval supplies, and the other to Alonzo de Morales, Treasurer, for money advanced to pay his traveling expenses from Granada to Seville.

There is also a copy of a letter he received from Dr. Toscanelli, a learned Florentine astronomer, some years before he started on his voyage, which confirms his theory of a western passage from Spain to the Indies. That is written upon the fly leaf of a book in his well-known hand, and is probably the oldest autograph in existence.

And, finally, there exists in Seville a volume of manuscript written partly by Christopher Columbus, partly by his brother Bartholemew, and partly by two amanuenses.

All of these autographs, except the Toscanelli letter, were written during the last years of his life, and most of them while Columbus was residing in the old monastery of Las Cuevas, on the outskirts of Seville, under the protection of the Carthusian friars. All of the manuscripts are so well preserved as to be easily photographed. His penmanship is firm, clear, and regular, in places even ornamental, although, under date of December 1, 1504, he tells Diego, "My illness prevents me from writing, except at night. In the day my hands have no strength." He was then about sixty years old.

The greater number of the autographs are the property of the Duke of Veragua, the present head of the Columbus family, who has also the original commission under which the memorable voyage of discovery was made, a number of royal orders concerning the preparations for that voyage, and several autograph letters addressed to Columbus by Ferdinand and Isabella, the sovereigns of Spain.

At the request of the Congress of the United States, expressed in a formal resolution, and conveyed to him through President Harrison, Veragua generously loaned the entire collection for exhibition in the Convent of La Rabida at the World's Columbian Exposition, and they furnished the most interesting historical exhibit there.

The letters and memoranda addressed to the sovereigns are in the archives of the Spanish Government. The other papers belong to the Columbian Library at Seville, the Municipal Government of Genoa, and to the Duke of Berwick and Alba, who also loaned his collection for exhibition at Chicago.

There are unsupported statements concerning letters and other autographs of Columbus in the possession of English collectors from fifty to a hundred years ago, but if they ever existed they have disappeared and no traces can be found of them.

Columbus was a very voluminous writer. Ninety-seven documents from his pen are known. He may have written many more, for his reputation in this respect was such as to cause the court jester of Charles V. to say that he and Ptolemy, the Egyptian geographer, "were twins in the art of blotting." Another contemporary, Zuniga, in a letter to the Marquis de Pescara, says: "God grant that Gutierrez may never come short for paper, for he writes more than Ptolemy, and more than Columbus, who discovered the Indies." Fortunately sixty-four of his compositions are preserved entire. They consist of letters descriptive of his plans, arguments and memoranda to sustain his theories concerning a western passage to the Indies, memorials to the court and appeals for justice, narratives of his voyage and personal correspondence. Some of his letters have never been printed. Several had never been translated into English until the preparation of this Monograph, and it may be a source of consolation to disappointed literary aspirants to know that a manuscript book by so eminent a man as he who discovered America has been awaiting a publisher for nearly four hundred years.

The least interesting of the manuscripts of Columbus, if offered for sale, would doubtless command a higher price than was ever yet paid for an autograph, and the enormous value that attaches to them has caused several clever forgeries of the Genoa document to be made. Some years ago an imitation of the letter to the Governors of the Bank of St. George was offered to the late Mr. S. L. M. Barlow, of New York, for the sum of two thousand dollars. He placed the matter in the hands of Mr. Henry Harrisse, the celebrated Columbian scholar of Paris, who very cleverly detected and exposed the forgery. He discovered that it was the work of an Italian rascal, who was afterwards condemned for theft and other crimes and committed to the prison of San Guiliano Persiceto in Genoa in 1885, under sentence of imprisonment for four years. It appears that the forger obtained from a book in the National Library at Paris blank sheets of vellum nearly of the exact size, age and texture as that upon which the genuine letter was written. Next, with a very soft lead pencil he blackened a sheet of ordinary thin paper on one side. This he tacked to the sheet of vellum, and having procured a photograph of the original pasted it upon the blank side of the paper. Then, with a pointed instrument he traced every letter and mark, which transferred a facsimile of the original to the vellum. Having removed the blackened page and the original he renewed the tracing with ink, chemically prepared so as to show age in the color.

A similar forgery, perhaps the same, is now in the possession of a New York gentleman, who undoubtedly believes in its genuineness; and, in 1892, fac-similes of all three of the Genoa letters, undoubtedly made in a similar manner, were sold to the President of Guatemala for a large sum of money, having been pronounced genuine by a committee of learned scholars in Spain.

During his memorable voyage of discovery Columbus kept a minute journal, but it has entirely disappeared. After his death his papers were stored in an iron chest in the Monastery of Las Cuevas, near Seville, where he was buried. The building is now used as a porcelain factory. After his body was removed to Santo Domingo about 1540, the chest and its contents remained in the possession of the Carthusian friars for seventy years or so, when, in 1609, they were delivered to Nuno de Portugal, who had been declared by the Council of the Indies the heir to his titles, privileges and estates. Meantime Bartholemew Las Casas, who was known as "the apostle to the Indies," had access to the documents in the preparation of his history of the Indies, and in that volume included a large portion of the journal, which was afterwards translated into English and published by Samuel

Kettell, in Boston, about 1832. What became of the original of the journal when Las Casas finished his work is unknown. It cannot be traced any farther than his hands.

Don Luis, the son of Diego Columbus, and the grandson of Christopher, was a worthless fellow, and after a career of adventures and dissipation was banished for bigamy to Africa, where he died, and the male line of the great discoverer became extinct seventy years after his death. Then began a series of law suits for the succession, which continued for two hundred and fifteen years until 1790, when the courts confirmed the claims of Don Mariano Colon de Toledo, the grandfather of the present Duke of Veragua, who was descended from the second son of Luis. In the meantime the family archives, including the precious papers that were exhibited at the World's Fair, were passed from one branch of the family to another, and many of them were lost.

The defeated claimant, Don Carlos Fernando Fitz-James Stuart, was a descendent of the youngest daughter of Luis Columbus. Some of his ancestors intermarried with the royal family of Stuarts of Scotland, and to him and to them the present Duke of Berwick-Alba traces his line. Several interesting autographs which were not transferred with the rest to the successful contestant are still in the possession of the latter gentleman, and were loaned for exhibition at Chicago. His wife, the present Duchess, a lady of rare accomplishments, has written a valuable history of the papers and published it at Madrid for private circulation. They include a memorandum prepared in 1504 by Christopher Columbus in support of his claims under his contract made with the sovereigns of Spain before the first voyage of discovery was undertaken; an autographic statement of the disposition of the gold he brought with him from Hispaniola on that voyage, and several drafts or orders for money which he desired paid to persons with whom he had business.

Both the Duke of Veragua and the Duke of Berwick-Alba have a full appreciation of the value of the papers, and preserve them in handsomely carved oaken chests.

One of the letters in the Duke of Veragua's collection, which was exhibited in La Rabida, is an original from the king of Portugal. It is believed that Columbus left Lisbon after the death of his wife to escape his creditors. The popular understanding, based upon his own statements, is that his departure was due to indignation at the action of the king in secretly sending an expedition into the western sea to ascertain the truth of his theory. But there is a record of his application to Prince John II, in 1488, two years later, for a passport to visit Lisbon to see his brother Bartholomew, who had just returned from an expedition to the Cape of Good Hope. This passport of safe conduct was necessary to protect him from arrest, and it will be seen from the answer, by the hand of the king himself, who writes with very good feeling, that Columbus feared both civil and criminal prosecution. This letter is as follows:

"We, Don Juan, by the grace of God, King of Portugal and the Algarbes, of the sea this side and the other of Africa, and of Guinea, do hereby send you a hearty greeting: We have read your letter, which made us acquainted with the good will and attachment you show through the whole of it towards us and for our service, and we are very grateful to you for your feelings. In regard to your coming here, we say that owing to what you indicate, and for other reasons, as well as for the desire of judging by ourselves of your industry and good talent, we shall thereby rejoice and be much pleased. And we say further that as far as we are concerned all things will be fixed in such a way as to give you full satisfaction. In order to avoid trouble when you reach, whether by virtue of circumstances or otherwise, any port or place under our jurisdiction, we give you by these presents free admission to all the said ports and places, and full permission to stay or leave, assuring you that you will not be molested in any way, or summoned or sued, whether civilly or criminally, for any cause whatever. And by means of this our Royal letter we do command all our tribunals and authorities to do as herein directed. Whereupon we pray you to come promptly and have no fear or apprehension whatever."

The Genoa autographs are perhaps the most interesting of all the relics of Columbus that remain. Before starting upon his fourth and last voyage in the spring of 1502, infirm in health and with impaired confidence in his sovereigns and the council of the Indies, Columbus had copies of all his contracts, privileges and commissions made and certified by the royal notary, and forwarded them to Nicolo de Oderigo, the Genoese Ambassador to the Spanish court, to be deposited with the Bank of St. George at Genoa, which was to the commercial world in those days what the Bank of England is to-day, and to be held in trust for the benefit of his heirs. He addressed the governors of that institution the following characteristic letter:

"Although my body is here my heart is always near you. Our Lord has bestowed upon me the greatest favor that He has ever granted to anyone except David. The results of my undertaking are already being seen, and would shine considerably if the darkness of the government did not conceal them. I shall go again to the Indies in the name of the Holy Trinity, and shall soon return. But as I am a mortal, I have ordered my son, Don Diego, to give you every year, forever, the tenth of all the revenues obtained, in payment of the taxes on wheat, wine and other provisions. If this tenth amounts to anything, please take it. If not, take my will for my deed. I ask you as a favor to attend to my said son Don Diego. Nicolo de Oderigo knows all about my letters of concessions and privileges, and I have asked him to take good care of them. I wish you would see them. The King and Queen, my sovereigns, wish to honor me now more than ever. The Holy Trinity may keep your noble persons in its keeping and increase the importance of your magnificent office."

He signs himself "The Great Admiral of the Ocean Sea, and Viceroy and Governor of the Islands and Mainland of Asia and the Indies belonging to the King and Queen, my sovereigns, The Captain General of the Sea, and a member of their Council."

Upon his return to Spain in 1504, having heard nothing from the Bank or from Oderigo about these documents, he writes an indignant letter which he signs "The Great Admiral of the Ocean, Viceroy and Governor General of the Indies, etc." He says:

"At about the same time of my departure from here, I sent to you by Francisco de Ribarol a book containing copies of several letters, and another in which all the grants and privileges given me were also copied, the whole inclosed in a red morocco case, with a silver lock. I also sent with the same man two letters to the St. George gentlemen, in which I assigned to them one-tenth of my revenues, in consideration of and compensation for the reduction made on the duties on wheat and other supplies. To nothing of this have I had any reply. Micer Francisco says that everything arrived safely. If this is the case, the failure of the St. George gentlemen to answer my letters is an act of discourtesy, for which the Treasury is by no means better off. This is the reason why it is generally said that to serve common people is to serve no one.

"Another book of my privileges, equal to the one above mentioned, was left by me at Cadiz with Francisco Catanio, (who is the bearer of this letter) with instructions to send it to you, in order that you would keep it together with the other, in some safe place, at your discretion."

The letters and documents sent by Columbus to the Bank of St. George were, however, duly entered upon the records of that institution, and the original may be seen in the handwriting of the chancellor on pages 256 and 257 of the manual for 1503. After the bank went into liquidation the precious documents, which are now referred to as the Codice Diplomatico, were transferred to the custody of the city authorities of Genoa, and are still preserved in what is called the "Custodia," a marble shaft surmounted by a bust of Columbus. There has recently been made, under the direction of the city government of Genoa, a beautiful fac-simile of the entire collection of papers.

The duplicate book which Columbus refers to as "My privileges equal (or similar) to the one mentioned above," which was left with Francisco Catanio with instructions to send it to Nicolo Oderigo in order that he might keep it with the first copy in some safe place, was taken by Napoleon I. from the municipal palace in Genoa when he captured that city in 1808. It was carried to Paris and deposited in the office of the Minister of Foreign Affairs, where it remains until this day. Mr. Benjamin Franklin Stevens, the well known American bookseller of London, has recently reproduced this historical volume with wonderful accuracy, and with copious and valuable historical notes.

All the writings of Columbus reflect his deep religious spirit, but now and then they show a glimpse of humor and a touch of human indignation. Before he commenced a letter or memoranda of any kind he always made the sign of the cross, with his pen, at the top of the sheet, and wrote an invocation. His son Fernando perpetrated an Irish bull when he said of his father:

"If he had anything to write he did not use his pen until he had first written these words, 'Jesus cum Maria sit nobis in vita,' and made the sign of the cross."

Las Casas says: "Whenever he writes a letter or any other document he always places at the top, 'Jesus cum Maria sit nobis in via.' Of his writings thus done with his own hand I now have in my possession a quantity."

Columbus usually closed his letters with the expression, "May God guard you in his holy keeping." In writing to the king and queen he says: "I shall ever pray to God, our Lord, to preserve the lives of Your Majesties, and enlarge your domains." Again: "May the Holy Trinity be pleased to give health to my Lady the Queen." Or again: "May the Holy Trinity preserve Your Highnesses as I wish and as we all need, with all your great estates and domains."

In a letter to Nicolo Oderigo, before departing upon his voyage he said: "I am ready to sail, with the favor of the Holy Trinity, as soon as the weather permits it," and from the Canary Islands he wrote to Father Gaspar at Seville: "Our Lord gave me such good weather that I arrived here in four days. Now I am going to continue my voyage in the name of the Holy Trinity and expect to succeed."

After hearing the news of the death of Queen Isabella, who was always his warmest friend and most ardent defender at court, he writes to Diego, his son: "The principal thing now is to commend to God affectionately and with much devotion the soul of our Lady, the Queen. Her life was always catholic and holy. She was always ready for the things of God's holy service, and for this it must be believed that she is in His holy glory and beyond all desires relative to this rough and tiresome world. Second, an effort should be made thoroughly and in all things to serve well the King, our Lord, and prevent him from being displeased. His Highness is the head of all Christendom. Remember the proverb that says that when the head aches all the members ache also. Therefore all good Christians must pray for the preservation of his health and for his being granted a long life."

In December, 1504, he writes to Diego: "I am living on what money I can borrow. The money I got there (in the Indies) was spent in bringing back to their homes the people who had gone with me, for it would have been a grave sin for me to leave them there unprotected. But Our Lord lives and he will fix everything as he knows to be the best for us."

In a letter to Diego, written from Seville on the 21st of November, the same year, he says: "My safe arrival and all the rest is in the hands of Our Lord. His mercy is infinite. Saint Augustine says that what is being done, or is about to be done, is a thing already done before the creation of the world."

"It is true that I served Their Highnesses with as much, or greater diligence and love as I might have displayed in trying to gain Paradise. If I failed to do something it was due either to the impossibility of the thing itself, or to its being entirely beyond my knowledge and my power. God, Our Lord, requires in such cases only the will."

In the same letter he refers to the fact that the brothers Porres, who mutinied and made him so much trouble when his vessel was wrecked at Jamaica, had been set free "by those who have charge of all the business of the Indies," and he observes: "I will not wonder if Our Lord punishes some one for this."

The recommendations of Columbus, to the sovereigns, concerning the management of affairs in the American colonies are sensible and practicable, although as an executive officer he proved a great failure. His preaching was better than his practice. In a letter written to Ferdinand and Isabella, in September, 1493, he says:

"And in order to secure the better and prompter settlement of the said islands, I should suggest furthermore that the privilege of getting gold be granted exclusively to those who have acquired a domicile and built a dwelling-house in the town of their residence, so as to persuade them all to live close to each other and be better protected.

"And further, that, whereas the extreme anxiety of the colonists to gather gold may induce them to neglect all other business and occupations, it seems to me that prohibition should be made to them to engage in the search of gold during some season of the year only so as to give all other business, profitable to the island, an opportunity to be established and carried on."

There is a paragraph in this letter which contradicts the general impression that Columbus was envious and jealous of other voyagers, and wanted to keep the Indies to himself, for he says: "As far as the business of discovering other lands is concerned, it is my opinion that permission to do so should be given to every one who desires to embark in it, and that some liberality should be shown in reducing the fifth to be paid as tribute, so as to encourage as many as possible to enter into such undertakings."*

In another letter, written subsequently, on the same subject, he makes a queer suggestion that the colonists be furnished with "salted flour, the salt to be mixed with the flour at the time it is milled."

The letters also give us a glimpse of his theology and philosophy. In a communication to the sovereigns of Spain, written from Granada, in 1502, he says:

"Sailors and other people who are conversant with the sea have always a better knowledge than all others of the parts of the world which they visit more frequently, or with which they do business oftener. Every one knows best what he sees every day, and what has happened lately is better known than what took place years ago. Hence it is that we hail with delight whatever is said to us by those who were eye witnesses of the facts, and no teaching proves to us more thorough and complete than that which comes to us through our own experience and observation.

"Whether we admit that the shape of the world is spherical, as many writers affirm it to be, or bow to the decision of science if its conclusion is different, the fact of the diversity of climate within the same zone must remain undisturbed. That diversity will be observed on land as well as on the sea.

"The sun exercises its influence on the earth, and the earth receives it in a greater or lesser degree, according to the character of its surface, whether mountainous or depressed. The ancients were well acquainted with this fact and wrote a good deal about it. Pliny went so far as to say that at the region of the North Pole, exactly at the same zone, the temperature is so mild that the people who inhabit the spot never die, unless they themselves, getting tired of living, put an end to their existence."

The little glimpses of human nature that we have now and then in his letters is quite amusing. For example, he writes to Diego, after the death of Isabella: "You must investigate whether the Queen, whom God hath in His glory, said something in her will about me."

Again, in a letter to Diego, referring to the indifference with which he was treated by the sovereigns, he says: "There is a proverb which saith that the eye of the owner maketh the horse fat. Here and there and everywhere, however, I shall serve Their Highnesses with pleasure as long as my soul remains united with my body."

---

* All persons who discovered or visited new lands were compelled to surrender as tribute to the Sovereigns of Spain one-fifth of all articles of value they brought home

In another letter he writes: "They say that Comancho and Master Bernal are anxious to go back there (that is, to Santo Domingo). They are two of those creatures for whom God hath made no miracles. If they go it will be to do harm rather than good, but they can do little because the truth will always prevail. This Master Bernal was the one who started the treasonable movement. He was arrested and charged with many crimes, for each of which he deserved to be quartered. At the request of your uncle and others he was pardoned, on the condition, however, that the pardon should be revoked and that he should be liable to punishment in the proper way if he said the slightest thing against me and my officers.

"As to Comancho, I will send you some legal papers. For more than eight days he has remained inside the church, without daring to leave it, for fear of the trouble in which he might get for his rashness and slanders. Diego Mendez is well acquainted with Master Bernal and his doings. The governor wanted to put him in prison while at Hispaniolo, but at my request he left him free. They say that he killed two men there with poison in revenge for some wrong which did not amount to three beans."

In 1504 he writes to Diego: "The caravel whose mast was broken when leaving Santo Domingo, has arrived. She brings the record of the investigation in the Porres matter. So many ugly things and such a display of cruelty as will be shown there has never before been seen. If Their Highnesses do not inflict the proper punishment I do not know how any person will ever dare to go abroad again to serve them."

He writes again to Diego: "It seems to me that a good copy should be made of that portion of the letter which Their Highnesses wrote to me, in which they promise to fulfill their engagements with me and give possession of everything to you, and that the copy be delivered to Their Highnesses, together with a statement in writing, explaining my sickness and the impossibility in which I am now prevented to go and kiss their royal hands and feet, and saying also that the Indies are going to ruin, and as if they were on fire on every side."

Diego Columbus was intended for the church. After the death of his mother in Portugal he came to Spain with his father, and when Columbus asked for bread and water at the gate of La Rabida he was on his way to the neighboring town of Moguer, where a sister of his wife, named Señora Mulier, was living, with whom he intended to leave the boy while he went into the interior to present his plans and theories to the sovereigns of Spain. It is supposed that Diego remained at La Rabida, in charge of the monks, while his father was following the court during the eight long years that passed before he finally received his instructions to make the memorable voyage, although there is no evidence except a tradition among the Franciscan fathers that he was educated at the convent.

The next we hear of him is his appointment as a page to Prince Juan, the son and heir of Ferdinand and Isabella, shortly before the departure of Columbus on his first voyage. After the death of the young prince Diego remained at the court, first as a page to Isabella, and then as a courtier, leading a useless and dissolute life.

In his will Columbus made Diego his sole heir, but imposed upon him many pious injunctions and obligations. To most, if not all of them, however, Diego was totally indifferent, and although while he was in the train of Ferdinand he did little or nothing to secure the rights of his father or relieve his distress, within twelve days after the death of the admiral we find Diego importuning the king for the official recognition of himself and the pecuniary dues for which Columbus had so long and persistently appealed. Ferdinand permitted him to bring a suit in the courts to establish the claims of the Columbus family against the crown of Spain, and it was decided in favor of Diego, but not until after his marriage to Doña Maria de Toledo, a cousin of the king, and a member of the most influential family at court, was the verdict satisfied, and even then only partially.

Columbus had a profound fondness for Diego, and wrote him long and affectionate letters while he was absent on his several voyages, but the frivolities of court life seemed to have absorbed the attention of the young man, and we find his father frequently complaining of a lack of affection for himself, as well as for his brother Fernando. There is a great deal of pathos in the letters of Columbus to his son, but the latter, engaged by the allurements and dissipations of the court, paid little attention to his poor old father, who, broken in health and spirits, was passing the last unhappy years of his life under the shelter of the friendly monastery at Seville. "I should like to have letters from you every day," he writes in December, 1504, "Your father loves you more than himself." Columbus refers to him as "My dearest son, Diego, by whom it pleases me to hear that His Highness is well served." Again he reproaches Diego for his indifference to his uncle Bartholomew, and says: "I beg you to pay to your uncle that respect which is due to him." Again he says: "How grieved I feel when I see that everybody here receives letters and that I who have so many of my people there do not receive any." In April, 1502, he says: "Since your letter of the 15th of November I have heard nothing from you. I wish that you would write to me very often. I should like to receive a letter from you every hour. Reason must tell you that I could not have a better source of relief from my afflictions. Many are the messengers who reach here every day, and the information they bring is such as to make my hairs stand on end." Again he says: "I am astonished at not receiving any letter from you above all others, and this astonishment is shared by all who are acquainted with me. Everybody else here has letters, but I, entitled more than all to expect them, receive none."

The confidence Columbus placed in his son Fernando is quite as conspicuous as his lack of faith in Diego, for he writes, saying: "To make your efforts (that is, Diego's attempt to secure justice for his father, from the king and queen) more efficient I have decided to send to you your brother, who, although a child in days, is not a child in understanding." Again he writes: "Take good care of your brother. He has a very good dispositon, and is no longer a boy. If you had ten brothers their number would not be too large. I have never found better friends under all circumstances than my brothers."

It appears that Diego did not treat his half brother with very much respect or affection, for we find his father admonishing him again: "Treat your brother as an elder brother should treat the younger. You have no other brother, and the Lord must be blessed for having made him such a good one. He has proved and continues to be a person of very clear head."

Now and then in his letters Columbus gives a bit of family gossip and on November 28, 1504, he writes Diego: "Your uncle has been very sick and is still suffering a good deal with tooth-ache and some trouble with his jaws."

In December, 1504, he writes: "Don Fernando left here with 150 ducats, to be expended at his discretion. He will have to use some part of that money, but he will give you whatever he can. He also carries with him a letter of credit upon some of your merchants there. You must be careful in this matter, because I have already had some trouble with the governor. Everybody told me that I had there some eleven or twelve thousand castellanos, and the result was that I had only four thousand. He wanted to charge me with many things which I was not bound to pay, and I, trusting on the promises made by Their Highnesses, that restitution of everything should be ordered to be made to me, decided to allow him to go on with his charges. I was in hopes that some day I could call him to account for that. He is so overbearing that nobody who has money there dares to ask for it. Miguel Diaz and Velazquez dare not even mention the subject to him."

As his age and infirmities increased, the anxiety of Columbus to secure a recognition of his claims grew greater, and he expressed a desire to go to Valladolid, where the court was sitting. But he says that he had "fear to make the journey because the ailment that afflicts me is so bad and the cold weather aggravates it so much that it is possible that I might be left on the road or in some of the inns. Stretchers and all the other things were ready, but the weather became so formidable that nobody could think of traveling, and everyone said that it was better for a person so well-known as I am to attend to my health and not run any risk. My illness," he adds, "prevents me from writing except at night. In the day time my hands have no strength."

A few months later he writes to Diego saying that "if without being importunate a permit can be obtained for me to ride on muleback, I will try to go there (Valladolid) after the month of January." A few weeks later he notified Diego again of his desire to make the journey, and says: "If the permit to ride on muleback can be obtained without trouble I would be pleased, and then I would like also to have a good mule."

The application for this permit was made necessary by an order issued a few months previous prohibiting the use of mules in traveling, except by royal permission, on account of the difficulty of securing a sufficient number of animals for military purposes. Cardinal Mendoza had placed his litter at the disposal of the old sailor, but he preferred to go on muleback. It appears that the request of Diego was granted, for about two months after this letter was written the king issued the following curious order, dated at the city of Toro, February 23, 1505.

"Decree granting to Don Christopher Colon permission to ride on a mule saddled and bridled through any part of these kingdoms:

"The King: As I am informed that you, Christopher Colon, the Admiral, are in poor health, owing to certain diseases which you had or have, and that you cannot ride on horseback without injury to your health, therefore, conceding this to your advanced age, I, by these presents, grant you license to ride on a mule, saddled and bridled, through whatever parts of these kingdoms or realms you wish and choose, notwithstanding the law which I issued thereto; and I command the citizens of all parts of these kingdoms and realms not to offer you any impediment or allow any to be offered to you, under penalty of ten thousand maravedi in behalf of the treasury from whoever does to the contrary."

After many attempts to make a journey he was too weak to undertake, Columbus started in May, 1505, under the patient and affectionate care of his brother, Bartholomew, and reached Segovia, where the king was living, in the following August; but his cool reception by the King only increased his mortification and distress. His personal application for redress was quite as ineffective as his letters, and he sank in despair. On the 25th of August he made his will, which is a very long and comprehensive document, and then, from his bed, renewed his written appeals, not for himself, as he realized that his days were numbered, but in behalf of his son. He begged King Ferdinand to bestow upon Diego the honors he had won, and restore to him the rights and authority of which he had been deprived.

The house at Valladolid, Spain, in which Columbus died, May 20, 1506, is still standing, and is visited by multitudes of tourists. At the time of his death it was an inn. His brother, Bartholomew, was with him. In none of the chronicles of the times, and they are numerous, is there any allusion to the event. It was not until nearly a month after that the fact was officially recorded, and then in the briefest and most indifferent manner. On the back of one of his belated appeals to the king some clerk wrote this endorsement:

"The within admiral is dead."

That is the only record in the archives of the Nation of the loss of him who brought Spain her greatest glory.

His letters written from Jamaica while on his voyage, in 1503, to Father Gáspar, show the same profound piety and the same loyalty to the sovereigns of Spain that appears in his other communications. " If my voyage could prove as conducive to my personal health and to the welfare of my house as it promises of aggrandisement to the royal crown of the King and Queen, my masters," he writes, "I might hope to live more than a thousand years;" and again from San Lucar he tells the "Reverend and Most Pious Father: If the anxiety to hear from you troubles me in the places where I am going as much as it does here I shall feel very badly."

While at Seville, in 1505, Columbus saw a good deal of Americus Vespucci. They had become acquainted in 1493, while the admiral was fitting out the ships for his second voyage; the contract for furnishing the supplies having been awarded to a merchant named Beradi, by whom Vespucci was employed, and the latter had active charge of the business. In the meantime Vespucci had himself made two voyages, cruising along a good deal of the northern coast of South America, and down the east coast as far as Bahia,

Brazil, where the Portuguese had established a trading post. It was at the conclusion of his second voyage, in September, 1504, that Americus wrote the account of his discoveries, which three years later, caused his name to be given to the New World; but there is no reason to believe that he anticipated or even hoped that his fame would be so closely linked to the western hemisphere. Nor is there any evidence of the slightest rivalry or jealousy between the two voyagers. On the contrary, on the 5th of February, 1504, Columbus writes from the convent of Cartuja, at Seville, to his son, Diego, as follows:

"Diego Mendez left here on Monday, the 3d of the present month. After he left I spoke with Amerigo Vespusze, the bearer of this letter, who goes there, where he has been called on the business of navigation. He always wanted to please me. He is a very honest man. Fortune has been as adverse to him as to many others, and his labors have not been so profitable to him as it was reasonable to expect. He goes for my good and is very anxious to do everything that may prove beneficial to me if it is within his power. I do not know of any particular thing in which I might instruct him to my benefit, because I do not know exactly what he is wanted for there. He goes determined to do for me all that he may possibly do. You must see what kind of service he may render to my advantage, and coöperate with him in having it rendered. He will work and speak and do everything suggested, but the suggestion must be made secretly, so as to remove suspicion."

After the death of his wife and his arrival in Spain, about 1486, Columbus fell in love with Beatriz Enriquez, a woman of good family, of Cordova. She was the mother of his son Fernando, and survived him, although nothing is known of her whereabouts during the time of his attendance at the court of Spain and while he was absent on his voyages. In his will the admiral directs his son Diego "to take care of Beatriz Enriquez, mother of Don Fernando, my son; supply her with all that can enable her to live in an honorable manner, she being a person to whom I am under such grave obligations; and do this to relieve my conscience, because it weighs heavily on my soul." That the family of Beatriz found no fault with her relations with Columbus is inferred from the fact that her brother commanded one of his ships during the third voyage.

Near the banks of the Guadalquiver river, on the outskirts of the city of Seville, a magnificent tree marks the place where stood the splendid abode of Fernando Columbus. This tree is said to have grown from a shrub brought from the New World by Christopher Columbus.

The mansion was long known as "The House of the Admiral,"

although there is no evidence that he ever lived in it; but it was occupied by Fernando Columbus for many years, and until his death.

Fernando was born about 1488. We know nothing about his early life, but in 1502, when the admiral sailed on his last voyage, he accompanied the expedition. Subsequently he was appointed a page at court, where he appears to have received a good education and acquired a literary taste. As a member of the retinue of Charles V he seems to have been a favorite with that monarch. Fernando traveled extensively in western Europe, and not only learned much by observation, but became an ardent collector of books in all languages. Oviedo describes him as a person of sweet dispostion, affable manners, and nobility of character.

Although Columbus in his will gave the greater portion of his estates to Diego, his legitimate son, King Ferdinand awarded to Fernando a considerable amount of land in San Domingo, and Charles V. gave him a generous pension, so that his income was more than $30,000 a year. There is no evidence that he ever married or had children, for at his death, in 1539, he left all his property, including a very large library, to his nephew Luis, the son of Diego Columbus. This library was one of the most notable collections of books in Europe, and is said to have contained twenty thousand volumes, which were mostly obtained between 1510 and 1537. Nearly every volume in the collection contained a memoranda giving the date and place of purchase, and affording a clue to the extent and direction of his travels. That he was a studious reader is shown by the copious annotations made upon the margins.

Don Luis Columbus, who was in Santo Domingo at the time, appears to have cared nothing for the books. He allowed them to pass into the control of the monks attached to the cathedral at Seville, and by royal command the manuscripts in the collection were placed in the national archives of Spain. Although Fernando left a legacy for the care and increase of the library, the funds appear to have been diverted to other uses, and the precious volumes were neglected until 1832, when it was found that the principal of the legacy had entirely disappeared and two-thirds of the books were missing. It was not until 1885, when Henry Harrisse, the famous Columbian scholar, called public attention to the outrage, that the Spanish government ordered the library repaired and catalogued, and placed in proper shelter and custody at Seville. There is a catalogue of the collection in the handwriting of the owner, which shows that it was of inestimable value. It appears, also, that it contained a manuscript work on the New World by Fernando himself, but that has disappeared with many other priceless manuscripts and printed volumes.

Fernando Columbus is buried in the cathedral, in Seville, and the resting place of his bones is covered by a tablet bearing an inscription, of which the following is a translation:

"Here rests the most magnificent Señor Don Fernando Colon, who applied and spent all his life and estate in adding to letters, and collecting and perpetuating in his city all his books, of all the sciences which he found in his time, and reducing them to four books. He died in this city, on the 12th of July, 1539, at the age of fifty years, nine months, and fourteen days. He was son of the valiant and memorable Señor Don Christopher Colon, the first admiral, who discovered the Indies and the New World, in the lifetime of Their Catholic Majesties, Don Ferdinand and Donna Isabella, of glorious memory, on the 11th of October, 1492, with three galleys and ninety people, having sailed from the port of Palos on his voyage of discovery, on the 3d of August previous, and returned to Castile with victory, on the 7th of March the following year. He returned afterward twice to people that which he had discovered. He died at Valladolid on the 20th day of May, 1506, aged ....
'Entreat the Lord for them."

Beneath this, in a circle, is a globe, presenting the western and part of the eastern hemisphere, surmounted by a pair of compasses. Within the border of the circle is inscribed:

"A Castilla y á Leon.
Mundo Nuevo dió Colon."

In the Columbina Library, as it is called, at Seville, which formerly belonged to Fernando Columbus, are a number of books which were carried by Christopher Columbus on his various voyages, and contain copious marginal notes in his handwriting. These books, in the order of their ages, are:

First. A copy of the Historia Rerum Ubique Gestarum, by Enea Silvio Piccolomini, afterwards Pope Pius II. A small folio volume printed at Colonia in the year 1477.

Second. The astronomical and cosmographical treatise of Cardinal Pedro de Alliaco, entitled "Imago Mundi," a gothic edition in folio, without date or imprint, but supposed to have been printed by Juan de Westphalia, at Lovaina, between the years 1480 and 1483.

Third. The Works of Marco Polo. Latin edition of 1484.

Fourth. "Historia Naturale de C. Plinio Secondo Tradocta di Lingua Latina in Fiorentina per Christophoro Landino Fiorentino al Serenissimo Ferdinando Re di Napoli." Published at Venice, September 11, 1489.

Fifth. "Alamach Perpetuus Cuius Radix est Annum 1473," by Abraham Zacuth, astronomer to King Don Manuel of Portugal. Printed in Leiria in 1496. It was this very book that Columbus used to predict the eclipse of the moon which so terrified the Indians in Jamaica that they became obedient to him, and furnished his party food. On the margins are calculations in his penmanship which were doubtless made to verify those of Zacuth.

Sixth. "Vidas de los Illustres Varones," by Plutarch, translated into Spanish by Alfonso de Palencia,—two large folio volumes printed in Seville in 1491, by Paolo de Colonia. They contain frequent marginal notes.

Seventh. "Concordantiæ Bibliæ Cardinalis S. P." A manuscript of the fifteenth century, containing 112 parchment leaves.

It is evident that Columbus consulted this manuscript frequently while preparing his "Libro de los Proficias," for on the margins are frequent cross references in his handwriting, various lines are underscored, and index fingers point to passages which were considered by him of peculiar signficance. It is claimed by some that this Concordance was prepared by Columbus himself, but there is no evidence of that fact, and, if so, the existing copy was made by an amanuensis. The four volumes last named have been discovered only recently among the books of Don Fernando Columbus, by Doctor Simon de la Rosa y Lopez, the librarian of the Columbina Library, and are considered of the highest importance.

The "Libro de las Proficias" is a volume of manuscript containing seventy leaves of vellum, although there appear originally to have been eighty-four. Fourteen seem to have been cut out of the center. It was prepared in the year 1504-5, and was scarcely completed at the time of the death of Columbus, its object being to demonstrate that his discoveries were predicted by the Holy Scriptures. It is a collection of various papers and memoranda, often incoherent, including a collection of texts from both the Old and New Testaments, that in his opinion refer to the existence of the lands he discovered, and their future conversion to Christianity. There are many marginal notes which would indicate that the manuscript is unfinished or at least that Columbus obtained additional material after completing it.

The first leaf begins with the usual pious invocation that proceeds all of his manuscripts and the sign of the cross. This is followed by a letter addressed by him from Granada to his friend Father Corricio at the Convent of Las Cuevas, on the 13th of September, 1501, concerning references by sacred and profane writers to the regions he had discovered, and also to the probability of the recovery of the Holy Land from the infidels. The answer of the monk, dated at the Monastery of Las Cuevas on the 23rd of March, 1502, is also inserted. Then follow various memoranda relating to the same subject, part of

AUTHENTIC LETTERS OF COLUMBUS.

it in the handwriting of Columbus, but the greater portion having been written by several different amanuenses. The penmanship of his brother Bartholomew and his son Fernando are identified in several places.

The signature or rubric of Columbus which appears at the close of all his communications, as the sign of the cross appears at the beginning, has never been satisfactorily interpreted. It was the custom in his time for men of importance to adopt sign manuals of a peculiar sort, as they adopted mottoes for their escutcheons, which had some apparent or concealed significance. The signs used by Columbus

S.
S. A. S.
X. M. Y.
Xpo Ferens.

are generally interpreted to mean "Servus Suplex Altissimi Salvatoris Christus Maria Vosef," which in English reads, "The humble servant of Christ, the Supreme Savior, Mary and Joseph, Christbearer." Others render it in Spanish, "Servidor Sus Altezas, Secras Christo Maria, Ysabel," which means, "I am the servant of their three Highnesses, the Sacred Christ, Mary and Isabella, Christ-bearer." The last line was often written "Christo Ferens," and several signatures appear without it, and with "El Almirante," (the Admiral) instead. These were written after his appointment as admiral in the Spanish navy. The most plausible rendering of the signs seems to be, "Salvo Sanctum Supulcrum Xriste Maria Yesus Xristo Ferens."

The following translations, made by Señor Doctor Jose Ignatio Rodrigues, Spanish Secretary of the Bureau of the American Republics, include all of the manuscripts of Columbus existing; arranged in the order of the dates at which they are supposed to have been written:

TRANSLATIONS.

I.

LETTER FROM COLUMBUS TO FERDINAND AND ISABELLA CONCERNING THE COLONIZATION OF THE ISLAND OF HISPANIOLA. WRITTEN BETWEEN JULY 5TH AND SEPTEMBER 25TH, 1493, BEFORE STARTING ON HIS SECOND VOYAGE. ORIGINAL IN THE ARCHIVES OF THE SPANISH GOVERNMENT.

Most High and Powerful Sirs:

In obedience to what Your Highnesses command me, I shall state what occurs to me for the peopling and settling of the Hispaniola Island and of all others, whether already discovered or hereafter to be discovered, submitting myself, however, to any better opinion.

In the first place, and in regard to the Hispaniola Island, I should suggest the number of settlers who may be found willing to go there to be up to two thousand, so as to render the possession of the country safer, and cause it to be more profitable. This will aid also in facilitating intercourse and dealing with the neighboring islands.

I suggest further three or four towns to be founded at convenient places, and the new settlers or colonists to be properly distributed among said towns.

And in order to secure the better and prompter settlement of the said island, I should suggest furthermore that the privilege of getting gold be granted exclusively to those who have acquired a domicile, and built a dwelling-house in the town of their residence, so as to secure for them all to live close to each other and be better protected.

And also that each town be given, as is customary in Castile, a mayor and a clerk.

And furthermore, that a church be built, and that secular priests or friars be sent there for the administration of the sacraments, the conversion of the Jews, and the proper worshiping of the Divinity.

And further, that no colonist be allowed to go and gather gold unless with a permit from the governor or mayor of the town in which he lives, to be given only upon his promising under oath to return to the place of his residence and faithfully report all the gold which he may have gathered, this to be done once a month, or once a week, as may be ordered of him, the said report to be entered on the proper registry by the clerk of the town in the presence of the mayor, and if so deemed advisable, in the presence of a friar, or secular priest, selected for the purpose.

And further, that all the gold so gathered be melted right away, and weighed and stamped subsequently with such a mark or seal as the town may have devised and selected; and that the share of that gold which belongs to Your Highnesses be given and delivered to the mayor of the town, the proper record thereof being made by the clerk, and by the secular priest or friar who may witness to it, so as to cause the transaction to be known by more than one person, and render the concealing of the truth impossible.

Furthermore, that all the gold which may be found without the mark or seal aforesaid in the possession of anyone who formerly had reported once as aforesaid, be forfeited and divided by halves, one for the informer and the other for Your Highnesses.

And further, that one per cent. of all the gold gathered be set apart and appropriated for building churches, and providing for their proper furnishing and ornamentation, and to the support of the secular priests or friars having them in their charge, and, if so deemed advisable, for the payment of some compensation to the mayors and clerks of the respective towns, so as to cause them to fulfill their duties faithfully; and that the balance be delivered to the governor and treasurer sent there by Your Highnesses.

And further, and in regard to the division of the gold and the setting apart the share which belongs to Your Highnesses, I am of the opinion that the operation must be entrusted to the said governor and treasurer, because the amount of the gold found may sometimes be large and sometimes small, and if so deemed advisable, that the share of Your Highnesses be established for one year to be one-half, the other half going to the gatherers, reserving for a future time to make some other and better provision if necessary.

And further, that if the mayors and clerks commit any fraud in these matters, or consent to it, the proper punishment be inflicted upon them, and that a penalty be likewise imposed upon those colonists who do not report in full the whole amount of the gold which is in their possession.

And further, that a treasurer be appointed and sent to the said island, who shall receive all the gold belonging to Your Highnesses, and shall have a clerk to make and keep the proper record of the receipts, and that the mayors and clerks of the respective towns be given proper vouchers for everything which they may deliver to the said treasurer.

And further, that whereas the extreme anxiety of the colonists to gather gold may induce them to neglect all other business and occupations, it seems to me that prohibition should be made to them to engage in the search of gold during some season of the year, so as to give all other business, profitable to the island, an opportunity to be established and carried on.

And further, that as far as the business of discovering other lands is concerned, it is my opinion that permission to do so should be given to every one who desires to embark in it, and that some liberality should be shown in reducing the fifth to be given as tribute, so as to encourage as many as possible for entering into such undertakings.

And now I shall set forth my opinion as to the manner of sending vessels to the Hispaniola Island, and the regulation of this subject which must be made, which is as follows: That no vessels should be allowed to unload their cargoes except at one or two ports designated for that purpose, and that a record should be made of all that they carry and unload; and that no vessels should be allowed either to leave the island except from the same ports, after a record has been made also of all that they have taken on board, so that nothing can be concealed.

And further, and in regard to the gold to be brought from the Island to Castile, that the whole of it, whether belonging to Your Highnesses or to some private individual, must be put in a safe, with two keys,—one to be kept by the master of the vessel, and the other by some person chosen by the governor and the treasurer, and that an official record be made of everything put in the said safe, in order that each one may have what is his, and that whatever gold, much or little, found there, in excess of what the record shows, be forfeited to the benefit of Your Highnesses, so as to cause the transactions to be made faithfully.

And further, that all vessels coming from the said island must come to unload to the Port of Cadiz, and that no person shall be allowed to leave the vessels, or get in them, until such person or persons of the said city as may be appointed for this purpose by Your Highnesses have boarded the same vessels, and received information from the masters of all that they have brought, and the official statement of the nature and value of the cargoes, so as to facilitate a thorough examination and find out whether anything has been brought hidden and not declared in the manifests at the time of shipment.

And further, that the said safe where the gold belonging to all may be placed and brought to Cadiz must be opened in the presence of the judicial authority of the said city, and of an officer appointed for that purpose by Your Highnesses, and that thereupon each one must be given what belongs to him.

May Your Highnesses keep me in their minds, while I, on my part, shall ever pray to God our Lord to preserve the lives of Your Highnesses and enlarge their dominions.

S.
S. A. S.
X. M. Y.
Xpo Ferens.

Sent by the Admiral.

II.

LETTER FROM COLUMBUS TO FERDINAND AND ISABELLA CONCERNING SUPPLIES FOR AND THE GOVERNMENT OF THE INDIES. WITHOUT DATE, BUT PROBABLY WRITTEN BEFORE SECOND VOYAGE. ORIGINAL IN THE COLLECTION OF THE DUKE OF VERAGUA, MADRID.

Your Highnesses ordered a statement to be made of all the things required for provisioning the Indies, and according to my opinion what is needed is as follows:

First of all six ships, which shall carry four or five hundred men, which in my judgment are necessary to conquer the Hispaniola Island. There are already in the said Island four vessels, two of which belong to Your Highnesses, while the two others are owned by halves, one named La Niña, by Your Highnesses and myself, and the other, named La Vaquenos, by Your Highnesses and a widow residing at Palos. The two vessels which are therefore required to complete the total of six must be of one hundred and twenty tons burden, each, so as to supply the deficiency of the four others, which are small. And to purchase said vessels will prove cheaper than to charter them; and the sailors must be engaged for certain fixed wages, and not otherwise, so as to secure better and cheaper service.

And for the fitting out and provisioning the vessels, and providing for the support of the people on board, things must be done in this way, namely: One-third of the provisions must be hard tack, of good quality and well seasoned, and not old, because otherwise most of it will be lost. Another third must be salted flour, the salt to be mixed with the flour at the time it is milled. The other third must be wheat. But it is necessary to put also on board a provision of wine, and bacon, and sweet oil, and vinegar, and cheese, and peas, and lentils, and beans, and salted fish, and honey, and almonds and raisins, and also some fishing nets and hoops.

Pitch and oakum, and nails, and tallow, and iron, and hardware are things which are also required for the proper repair of the ships; and among the people on board the said ships there must be some who are calkers, and some who are carpenters, and coopers, and sawyers, and blacksmiths, and it will be cheaper to carry saws.

And it will be good for the ships sent there to carry sheep, and cows and goats, especially if they are young, said animals to be got at the Canary Islands, because those islands are nearer and the price will be cheaper there than elsewhere.

And it will be advisable to put on board some linen goods and broad-cloths for clothing purposes, and some shoes, and cotton, and needles, and bunting, and canvas and caps, and saddles and harness for the horses, and also spurs.

And furthermore it is necessary for the ships going to the islands, as well as for the people residing there, to be provided with Lombardy guns for the ships themselves, and with lances and swords, and daggers and crossbows and their appurtenances, and ammunition for the men.

And in reference to all those things which are required for the medical treatment of the sick Father Fray Juan will give Your Highnesses full information.

If the things above mentioned are to be given by lots, or rations, it will be necessary to entrust the distribution thereof to some person of good conscience; willing to give each one what is his, and incapable of depriving any one of what belongs to him. And if it is decided that the said things will not be distributed by lots or rations, then it will be necessary to give the people some part of their wages in money so as to enable them to purchase the said articles.

And then it will be likewise necessary to have there some one of good conscience, who will do justice to all, and give each one a fair treatment, because if those who are now in authority continue to exercise their power the inhabitants, Christians as well as Indians, will leave the country, for the treatment received by the former as well as by the latter is more in conformity with the dictates of cruelty than with the principles of reason and justice. And, as many of those who are there may be willing to domicile themselves in the island, it will be advisable for the one exercising authority in these matters to be provided with full powers to enter into arrangements, or to allow engagements to be released, as may be required.

S.
S. A. S.
X. M. Y.
Xpo Ferens.

III.

LETTER FROM COLUMBUS TO FERDINAND AND ISABELLA. DATED GRANADA, FEBRUARY 6TH, 1502. ORIGINAL IN THE ARCHIVES OF THE SPANISH GOVERNMENT.

Most High and Powerful Queen and King, my Lady and my Lord:

I wish I could give Your Highnesses pleasure and contentment, instead of burdening and annoying your minds. But as I know how great is the interest which Your Highnesses feel for all new things having some importance, I shall in obedience to your command set forth at this moment all that may come to my memory in regard to this subject, hoping that Your Highnesses will pardon the lack of ornament in my statements, and look only to my good intention. I am bold enough to say that as far as the good service of Your Highnesses is concerned I am not in need of learning from any one what I myself know well how to do; and if on any occasion it should happen for me to lose my strength, or to be overcome by fatigue, the will to serve Your Highnesses as your most dutiful servant will not nevertheless leave me for an instant.

Sailors and other people who are conversant with the sea have always a better knowledge than all others of the parts of the world which they visit more frequently, or with which they do business oftener. Every one knows best what he sees every day, and what has happened lately is better known than what took place years ago. Hence it is that we hail with delight whatever is said to us by those who were eye witnesses to the facts, and that no teaching proves to be for us more thorough and complete than that which comes to us through our own experience or observation.

Whether we admit that the shape of the world is spherical, as many writers affirm it to be, or bow to the decision of science if its conclusion is different, the fact of the diversity of climate within the same zone must remain undisturbed. That diversity will be observed on land as well as on the sea.

The sun exercises its influence on the earth, and the earth receives it in greater or lesser degree, according to the character of its surface, whether mountainous or depressed. The ancients were well acquainted with this fact and wrote a good deal about it. Pliny went so far as to say that at the region of the north pole, exactly at the same zone, the temperature is so mild that the people who inhabit the spot never die, unless they themselves, getting tired of living, put an end to their existence.

Here in Spain this diversity of temperature in the same zone is so perceptible that no testimony of ancient writers, or others, is required to prove it. Here in Granada we see the mountains capped with snow, which is a sign of great cold, during the whole year, and at the foot of these very mountains there are Alpujarras, where the temperature is delightful, neither too warm nor too cold. And what happens in this respect in this province happens also in many others of Spain, which it would be prolix to enumerate.

I say that on the sea the same things can be observed, especially in the proximity of the land; and this is known much better by those who frequent those waters than by the ones who travel elsewhere at a greater distance.

In Andalucia, it is taken for granted, during the summer, that each day, as soon as the sun has reached a certain height, a mild and soft breeze from the west, which they call "virazon," will commence to blow, and last until the evening. And what this "virazon" does for this region, other breezes of analogous character do for other regions sometimes in summer, sometimes in winter.

Those who frequently travel from Cadiz to Naples know well, according to the season, the kind of winds they will find when passing along the coast of Catalonia, or when entering the Gulf of Narbona. Travelers from Cadiz to Naples, if they make the trip during the winter, pass generally in sight of Cape Creo in Catalonia, and then through the gulf of Narbona; they will find there strong winds which they will do well to obey. These winds will push them to Berneria; and it is for this reason that the navigators go as near as they can to Cape Creo, so as to have as fully as possible the benefit of these winds, and promptly reach the Pomegas of Marseilles, or the Eres Island. From here they continue, always in sight of land, to whatever place they desire. If the trip from Cadiz to Naples is to be made in summer, it is made along the coast of Berneria up to Sardinia, and from there it will continue in the same way as before described. The men who are engaged in this navigation, and have made many trips, are well acquainted with these routes, and know what kind of weather they will meet, according to the season. In common parlance we call these men "pilots," which means "leaders," or "guides." But a man who is a very good guide, and knows well how to go from here to Fuentorrabia may be a bad guide and know nothing about the way to go from here to Lisbon. And the same thing happens on the sea, there being pilots who are excellent for the waters of Flanders, and others for those of the East, each one well fitted for the locality to which he is accustomed.

There is great intercourse between Spain and Flanders, and there are great sailors engaged in that navigation. In Flanders, in January, all the ships are ready to go back to their own countries, as it is rare that a wind from the northeast, which they must avoid, does not make its appearance soon after This wind which at this season is cold, and blows wildly, is often dangerous. It is due to the distance of the sun and to the quality of the land at that place. Fortunately, it does not blow regularly, or permanently, and allows some opportunity to escape it. But the navigator who trusts himself to the sea under such winds does so at a great risk, and often owes his safety only to being able, through some change in the direction of the wind to enter some French or English port, and wait there until the weather changes

Sailors are people who are fond of making money and of returning home, and under the spur of these two feelings are apt to venture all and not wait for the good weather, unless reluctantly. I, myself, as I have said to Your Highnesses on another occasion, once made this voyage, being forced to keep my bed on account of sickness, and when the sun had already left Taurus, and we were in the midst of a severe and dangerous winter. If the winds are favorable the distance is traveled quickly; but no one must start without being sure of the weather, and this assurance can be obtained by observing the sky, and finding out that this is very clear and that the wind comes from the side of the northern star, and blows for some days always in the same direction.

Your Highnesses know well what happened in the year 1497, while Your Highnesses were at Burgos, and the people were kept in such a state of anxiety on account of the severe storms which raged there continually one after another. The weather was so annoying that Your Highnesses decided to leave Burgos and go to Loria. In pursuance of this plan the whole court moved for the latter city on the appointed day, which was a Saturday, it being the intention of Your Highnesses to follow on the next Monday. But that very night Your Highnesses received a letter of mine in which I said: The wind began to blow on such and such a day, the fleet cannot have set sail that day, but must have waited until the weather settles, which probably has been on Wednesday. If the fleet started then, it will reach the Island of Huict on Thursday or Friday, and if it does not stop there it will enter Laredo next Monday, or all the sailors' calculations will prove to be false. This letter of mine, coupled with the desire of Your Highnesses to see the Princess sooner, caused Your Highnesses to abandon the idea of going to Loria, and put to test the opinion of the sailor. On Monday, indeed, one of the vessels which had refused to stop at Huict, because of the scarcity of her provisions, entered the port of Laredo.

Many predictions of this kind can be made, and in fact have always been made both on land and on the sea. They certainly will be repeated now, among the many who will navigate between here and the newly discovered islands. The route is known; but if the instruments as well as the rigging and equipment of the vessels are improved, those who will engage in this business will know moret han all others about those lands, and the winds and the times which are more suitable for their purposes, and for the safety of their persons.

May the Holy Trinity preserve Your Highnesses, as I wish and we all need, with all your great states and dominions.

Granada, February 6th, 1502.

S.
S. A. S.
X. M. Y.
Xpo Ferens.

Endorsement upon enclosure of No. III.
Memorial of the Admiral to Their Highnesses.
He came to Valladolid in the year of————

Facsimile of letter to Nicolo Oderigo, March 21st, 1502.

IV.

LETTER FROM COLUMBUS TO NICOLO ODERIGO. DATED SEVILLE, MARCH 21ST, 1502. ORIGINAL IN THE MUNICIPAL PALACE, GENOA.

Sir:

The loneliness in which you have left us cannot be described. I gave Francisco de Ribarol the book containing my deeds and other written documents in order that he may send it to you with another copy of the letters. I ask you as a favor to inform Don Diego of your action on this matter. A duplicate of everything will be made and sent to you, in the same way and by the same Francisco. You will see that in these papers there is a new deed. Their Highnesses have promised me, as you will see, to give me all that belongs to me, and to give possession of all to Don Diego. I have written to Juan Luis and Sra. Madona Catalina. My letter to them goes together with the present one. I am ready to sail, with the favor of the Holy Trinity, as soon as the weather permits it. I am well provided of everything. If Jeronimo Santiesteban is coming, he must wait for me, and not embarrass himself with anything. Otherwise they will take from him all that they can and leave him thereafter in the cold. Let him come here, and the King and the Queen will receive him and attend to him until I come.

Our Lord may keep you in His holy guard. Dated this 21st day of March, at Seville, 1502.

Command me.

S.
S. A. S.
X. M. Y.
Xpo Ferens.

Facsimile of letter to the Governors of the Bank of St. George, at Genoa, April 2nd, 1502.

V.

LETTER FROM CHRISTOPHER COLUMBUS TO THE GOVERNORS OF THE BANK OF ST. GEORGE, GENOA. DATED AT SEVILLE, APRIL 2ND, 1502.

Most Noble Lords:

Although my body is here my heart is always near you. Our Lord has bestowed on me the greatest favor which He has ever granted any one except David. The results of my undertaking are already being seen, and would shine considerably if the darkness of the government did not conceal them. I shall go again to the Indies in the name of the Holy Trinity, and shall soon return. But as I am a mortal, I have ordered my son Don Diego to give you every year, forever, the tenth of all the revenue obtained, in payment of the tax on wheat, wine and other provisions. If this tenth amounts to anything please take it. If not, take my will for my deed. I ask you as a favor to attend to my said son Don Diego. Nicolas de Oderigo knows all about my letters of concessions and privileges, and I have asked him to take good care of them. I wish you would see them. The King and the Queen, my sovereigns, wish to honor me now more than ever.

The Holy Trinity may keep your noble persons in its guard, and increase the importance of your magnificent office. Dated at Seville, this 2nd of April, 1502.

The Great Admiral of the Ocean Sea, and Viceroy and Governor of the Islands and Mainland of Asia and the Indies belonging to the King and Queen, my sovereigns, their Captain General of the Sea, and a member of their Council.

.S.
S. A. S.
X. M. Y.
Xpo Ferens.

Facsimile of letter to Father Gaspar de Las Cuevas, April 4th, 1502.

VI.

LETTER FROM COLUMBUS TO FATHER D. GASPAR AT SAN LUCAR, DATED APRIL 4TH, 1502. ORIGINAL IN THE COLLECTION OF THE DUKE OF VERAGUA, MADRID.

Reverend and Most Pious Father:

If the anxiety to hear from you troubles me in the places where I am going as much as it does here, I shall feel very badly. The equipments sent to me have been in such a large quantity that I have been compelled to leave a part. Everything will be done afterwards more at leisure. The Adelantado has already left with the ships to clean the bottom thereof at Puebla vieja. I shall sail in the name of the Holy Trinity Wednesday morning. Your Reverence will see Don Diego on his return, and will instruct him well in regard to a memorial of mine which I have left with him, and of which I should like Your Reverence to have a copy. Some one will go there for my little trunk in order to see some deeds, and the letter sent by me for that purpose I shall write it myself. Don Diego will take it to you with my regards. I commend myself to the pious members of your religious house, especially to the Reverend Father Prior, whose always willing servant I am. Dated April 4th.

All that Your Reverence may command will be done by

S.
S. A. S.
X. M. Y.
Xpo Ferens.

Facsimile of letter to Father Gaspar de Las Cuevas, September 4th, 1502.

VII.

LETTER FROM COLUMBUS TO FATHER D. GASPAR AT SEVILLE. MAY 1502. ORIGINAL IN THE COLLECTION OF THE DUKE OF VERAGUA, MADRID.

Reverend and Most Pious Father:

The wind from the east detained me in Cadiz (calis) until the day in which the Moors besieged Arzila, and I took advantage of that wind to go to the assistance of the besieged, and I was the first to do so. Subsequently to that Our Lord gave me such a good weather that I arrived here in four days. Now I am going to continue my voyage in the name of the Holy Trinity, and expect to succeed. I pray Your Reverence to remember to write often to Don Diego, and to remind Francisco de Rivarol of the business of Rome. I do not write to him, because I have no time. I commend myself to the Father Superior and to all the pious members of your religious house. We all here are well, thanks to Our Lord. Dated at Gran Canaria, on —— of May.

What Your Reverence may command will be done by

S.
S. A. S.
X. M. Y.
Xpo Ferens.

NOTE.—While the day of the month is erased in the original, the letter must have been written between the 20th and the 25th.

17. C. Letter of Columbus to Rev. Father de las Cuevas, dated July 7th, 1503.

Facsimile of letter to Father Gaspar de Las Cuevas, July 7th, 1503.

VIII.

LETTER FROM COLUMBUS TO FATHER D. GASPAR. DATED JAMAICA, JULY 7TH, 1503. ORIGINAL IN THE COLLECTION OF THE DUKE OF VERAGUA, MADRID.

Reverend and Most Pious Father:

If my voyage would prove as conducive to my personal health and to the welfare of my house as it promises of aggrandizement for the Royal Crown of the King and Queen, my masters, I might hope to live more than one hundred years. I have no time to write now more at length. I expect that the bearer of the present letter will be some one of my house who will give you verbally more information than can be given in a thousand letters. Don Diego will also supply it. I ask as a favor of the Father Superior and of all the members of your religious house to remember me in their prayers. Dated at the island of Jamayca (Janahica) on the 7th of July, 1503.

All that your Reverence may command will be done.

         S.
        S. A. S.
        X. M. Y.
       Xpo Ferens.

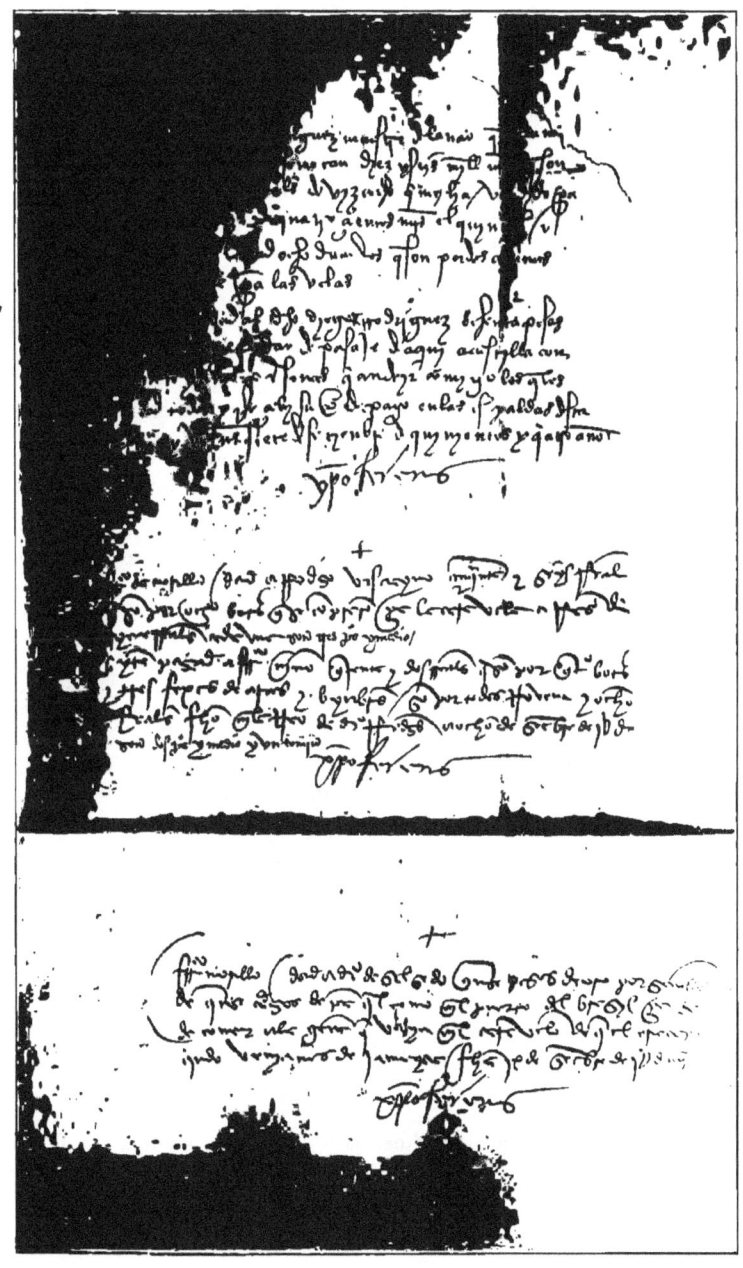

Facsimile of three letters to Francisco de Morrillo, Treasurer of the Crown,

IX.

LETTERS FROM COLUMBUS TO FRANCISCO DE MORILLO, PROBABLY TREASURER OF THE CROWN. ORIGINALS IN THE COLLECTION OF THE DUKE OF BERWICK-ALBA, MADRID.

Francisco de Morillo:

Give Diego Rodriguez, the master of the vessel, as he is called, as many gold dollars as are equivalent to sixteen thousand *maravedis* in payment of forty hundred weight of hard tack which he sold to me for the crew, at the rate of 400 *maravedis* the hundred weight. Give him furthermore, eight ducats in payment of two "alunas," which I bought from him for the sails. Give also the said Diego Rodriguez eighty gold dollars which I must pay him for his fare and that of the twenty-five persons who will go with him from here to Castile. Give him all of this and make him receipt for it on the back of this letter.

Dated to-day, Friday, the 7th of September, 1504.

Xpo Ferens.

X.

Francisco Morillo:

Give Rodrigo Viscayno fifty-six *reales*, in payment of eight "botas" (small wine skins), bought for the caravel at the rate of seven *reales* each. This makes three dollars and a half.

Give also Francisco Nino forty-two *reales*, in payment of four "botas" and three "fexes de aras y bimbres." This makes in all ninety-eight *reales*.

Dated on board the ship of Diego Rodriguez on the 8th of September, 1504.

Two dollars and a half and one *tomin*.

Xpo Ferens.

XI.

†

Francisco Morillo:

Give Diego de Salcedo fifteen gold dollars in payment of fifteen loads of bread which he took at the port in Brazil, when we were coming from Jamaica, to feed the people on board the ship of which he was the master.

Dated September 9th, 1504.

Xpo Ferens.

XII.

LETTER FROM COLUMBUS TO DIEGO, HIS SON. WRITTEN AT SEVILLE ON THE 21ST OF NOVEMBER (PROBABLY) 1504. ORIGINAL IN THE COLLECTION OF THE DUKE OF VERAGUA, MADRID.

†

My Dearest Son:

I received your letter which came by the post. You did well in remaining there, and attempting to remedy certain things and seeing already about your business. My Lord the Bishop of Palencia has always favored me, and wished for my being honored, ever since I came to Castile. Now is the time to request him to be pleased to look into the many wrongs which have been done to me and to cause my agreement with Their Highnesses and the letters of concession which Their Highnesses granted to me, to be ordered to be complied with, trying also to secure that a proper indemnification for so many injuries be paid to me. He must rest assured that if Their Highnesses do so their dominions and greatness will be increased in an incredible degree. He must not think forty thousand gold dollars too much, as a much greater sum might have been obtained, if Satan had not interfered to prevent my plans from being carried out, because when I was brought from the Indies the labors in which I was already engaged promised to give an amount of gold superior beyond comparison to forty thousand dollars. I can state upon oath, and this I say to you alone, that the injury done to me in the matter of the concessions which Their Highnesses granted me amounts to ten millions per year, which never will be recovered. Now imagine what will be the injury done to Their Highnesses themselves for the share in said concessions which belongs to them. But they do not feel it. I write as one who is at their mercy, and shall make an effort to leave for there. My safe arrival and all the rest is in the hands of Our Lord. His mercy is infinite. Saint Augustine says that what is being done, or is about to be done, is a thing already done before the creation of the world. I have also written to those other gentlemen named in the letter of Diego Mendez. Commend me to their mercy and inform them of my intended voyage there, as I said before. Indeed I am afraid of being unable to reach my destination, and be left on the roadside, on account of the cold weather, which is unfavorable in such a great degree to this illness of mine.

I was very much pleased with your letter and with what the King Our Lord said, and for which I suppose you kissed his royal hands. It is true that I have served their Highnesses with as much, or greater, diligence and love as I might have displayed in trying to gain paradise. If I failed to do something it was only due either upon the impossibility of the thing itself, or upon its being entirely beyond my knowledge and my power. God, Our Lord, requires in such cases only the will.

At the request of Treasurer Morales I made there two appointments in favor of two brothers named Porres. I made one of them a Captain and the other an Auditor. Neither of them had ability to fill his position; but I, in the desire to provide those places, and through love to the person who recommended them, made the appointments. Both men soon turned vainer than they had ever been. I overlooked more acts of theirs' than I had done for my relatives, and they were such as to deserve graver punishment than a simple verbal reprimand. They went to such an extreme as not to allow me, even if I had been willing, to change the decision which I reached. The record of the case will prove what I say. They revolted in the island of Jamaica, and I was as astonished by their actions as I had been by seeing the light of the sun turned into darkness. I was then almost at the point of death, and they made me suffer cruelly, without any cause for it, for no less than five months. At last I made them all prisoners, but afterwards I set them all, except the Captain, at liberty. I desired to bring the Captain as a prisoner before Their Highnesses. A petition, made upon oath, which was addressed to me and which I forward to you with this letter, will give you full information about this affair, although the record of the case will better explain the whole thing. That record and the clerk who attended it are coming in a vessel whose arrival I am expecting from day to day. The said prisoner was kept and retained in Santo Domingo by the Governor. His punctiliousness compelled him to do so. There was a provision in my introduction by which all were commanded to obey my orders, and full jurisdiction was granted me in civil and criminal cases concerning all those who had come with me. But this provision was of no avail with the Governor, because he said that it was not meant for his district, and was not applicable to it. Afterwards he sent him here without record or anything in writing to the Lords who have charge of all the business of the Indies; but they did not receive him and both brothers are free. I will not wonder if Our Lord punishes some one for this. They went there as unprincipled and shameless as ever. Such an act of jealousy and treason as this was never heard of before. I wrote to Their Highnesses about this matter and I said to them that it was not right for them to consent to such a slight to me. I also wrote to the Treasurer and asked him, as a favor, not to pass his sentence upon words which they might say to him without giving me a hearing. Now it will be right for you to remind him of my request. I do not know how they will dare to go before him with such a scheme. I have written to him again, and enclosed a copy of

Facsimile of portion of letter to Don Diego Columbus, November 21st, 1504.

the sworn statement, which I send to you, and also to Doctor Angulo, and Licenciate Zapata. I commend myself to the mercy of them all, and give them notice that in a short time I shall leave for there.

I would be happy to see a letter of Their Highnesses and know through it what they command me to do. You must try, if you have an opportunity, to get such a letter for me. Present my compliments to the Bishop, and also to Juan Lopez, and remind them of my illness and of the reward due for my services.

You must read the other letters that go with the present, so as to be able to act in conformity with what they say.

Tell Diego Mendez that I am obliged to him for his letter. I do not write to him, because he will know through you all that has passed, and because my illness precludes me from doing it. At this time it would be well for Carbajal and Jeronimo to be in the Court, and speak of our business with those Lords and with the Secretary.

Dated at Seville, on the 21st of November.

Your father who loves you more than himself.

.S.
.S. A. S.
X. M. Y.
Xpo Ferens.

I wrote to Their Highnesses requesting them to cause the people who went with me to be paid. They are poor and have been for three years away from their homes. The information that has reached them is more than extraordinary. They have run a great many dangers and experienced a great many difficulties. I did not want to plunder the country in order not to give scandal. Reason advises that an effort be made to bring population to the country, and then all the gold desired will be got without scandal. Speak of this to the Secretary and to the Bishop, and to Juan Lopez, and to whomever you may think to be advisable.

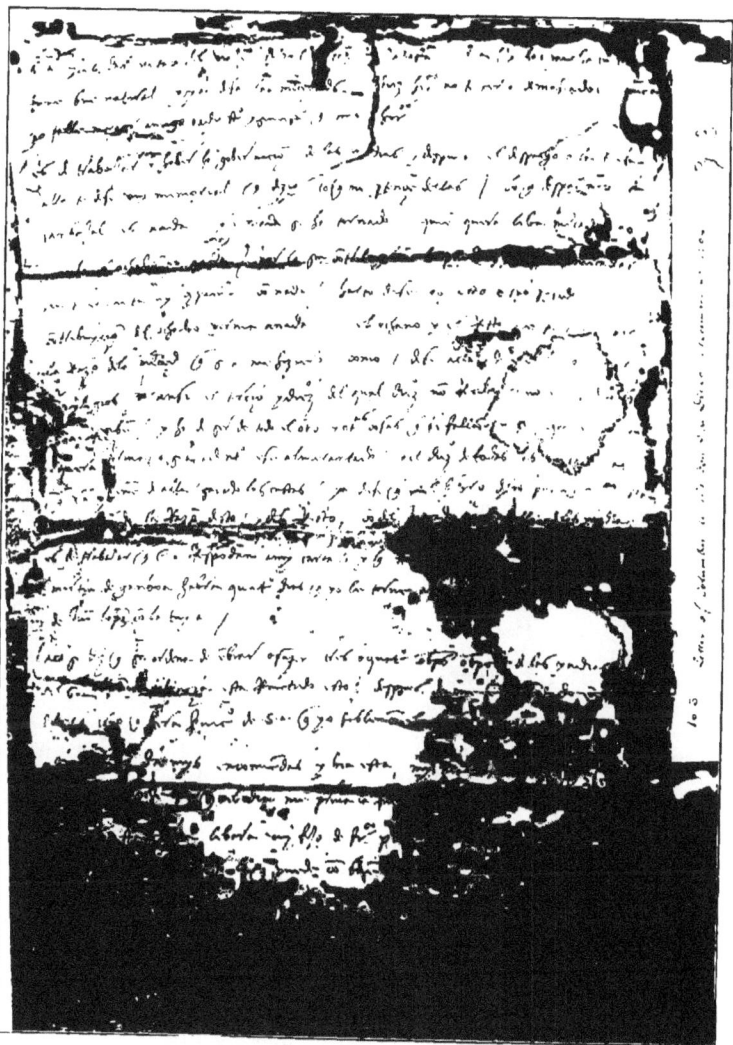

Facsimile of portion of letter to Don Diego Columbus, November 29th, 1504

XIII.

LETTER FROM COLUMBUS TO DIEGO, HIS SON. WRITTEN FROM SEVILLE, NOVEMBER 29TH, 1504. ORIGINAL IN THE COLLECTION OF THE DUKE OF VERAGUA, MADRID.

My dearest son:

    I received your letter of the 15th instant. I wrote to you eight days ago, and I sent the letter by a messenger. I enclosed in my letter some others addressed to other persons, which I did not seal in order that you could read them and subsequently have them sealed and delivered. Although this illness of mine gives me much trouble, still I am getting ready to start on my voyage there. I am very anxious to have an answer from Their Highnesses, and I wish you would try to get it. I wish also Their Highnesses would provide for the payment of those poor people who have gone through such incredible ordeals and have rendered them so great services, for which they must give infinite thanks to God, Our Lord, and greatly rejoice. If I .... the Paralipomenon, the Book of Kings, the Antiquities of Josephus, and other books will say what they know about it—I expect, trusting in Our Lord, to leave here next week, and for this reason it will be better for you not to write so often. I have not heard from Carbajal or Jerome. If they are there give them my regards. Times are such as to require both Carbajals to be in the Court, unless prevented by illness. Give my regards to Diego Mendez. I think that his true statements and his activity will outweigh the lies of the Porres. The bearer of this letter is Martin de Gamboa, who also carries a letter to Juan Lopez and a letter of credit. Read the letters to Lopez and then return it to the bearer. If you write to me, send the letter to Luis de Soria, who will make them reach me wherever I may be. I believe that if I go I shall be carried on a stretcher, on account of my illness. May Our Lord keep you in his holy guard. Your uncle has been very sick, and is still suffering a good deal with toothache and some trouble in the jaws.

    Dated at Seville, this 29th of November.

    Your father who loves you more than himself.

S.
S. A. S.
X. M. Y.
Xpo Ferens

Facsimile of portion of letter to Don Diego Columbus, December 1st, 1504.

XIV.

LETTER FROM COLUMBUS TO HIS SON DIEGO. WRITTEN AT SEVILLE ON THE 1ST DAY OF DECEMBER, 1504, ORIGINAL IN THE COLLECTION OF THE DUKE OF VERAGUA, MADRID

My dearest son:

Subsequent to your letter of the 15th of November, I have heard nothing from you. I wish you would write to me very often. I should like to see a letter from you every hour. Reason must tell you that now I could not have a better relief. Many are the messengers that reach here every day, and the information they bring is such as to make my hair stand on end, seeing how things are going so much against my wishes. May the Holy Trinity be pleased to give health to the Queen, Our Lady, that she may settle and affirm what has been built. Last Thursday I wrote to you by a messenger, who, I suppose, is now on his way back to this place. I told you in that letter that my departure from here was a sure thing, but that my safe arrival there was, on the contrary, and judging from experience, extremely uncertain. The ailment which afflicts me is so bad, and the cold weather aggravates it so much, that it is very possible for me to be left on the road in some of the inns. The stretchers and all other things were ready. But the weather became so formidable that nobody could think of traveling, and all said that it was better for a person so well known as I am to attend to my health and not to run such great risks. I told you also in that letter, as I now say again, that it was a good thing for you to stay where you are, specially at this time, and that it was advisable for us to begin to look into our affairs. Reason advises us to do so. It seems to me that a good copy must be made of that chapter of the letter which Their Highnesses wrote to me, in which they promise to fullfill their engagements with me and give possession of everything to you,.... and that said copy must be delivered to Their Highnesses, together with a statement in writing, explaining my sickness and the impossibility in which I am now to go and kiss their royal hands and feet, and saying also that the Indies are going to ruin, and are as if they were on fire one very side; that I have received nothing of the revenue which I should get from there; that no person dare make any demands in my favor, and that I am living on the money that I can borrow. The money which I got there was spent in bringing back to their homes the people who had gone with me, for it would have been a grave sin for me to leave them there unprotected. Information of this step must be given to the Bishop of Palencia, in whom I trust so much, and also to his chamberlain. I had thought that Carbajal and Jerome were still at your place. But our Lord is there and He will fix everything as He knows to be the best for us.

Carbajal reached here yesterday. I wanted to send him back at once with this very instruction; but he asked to be excused, on the ground that his wife is at the point of death. I shall see that he goes as soon as possible, because he knows much about this business. I shall endeavor, also, to send your brother and your uncle to kiss the hands of Their Highnesses, and make a report of the voyage, if the one made in my letters is not sufficient. Take good care of your brother. He has a very good disposition, and is no longer a boy. If you had ten brothers their number would not be too large. I never found better friends, under all circumstances, than my brothers.

We have to work first in fixing such matters as are relating to the government of the Indies, and subsequently in the straightening out the business of our revenue. I gave you a memorandum in which I stated all that belongs to me. What they awarded Carbajal is nothing and has returned into nothingness. Whoever wishes to take there any merchandise can take it, and therefore the eighth becomes nothing. I might send there any kind of merchandise and sell it without entering into accounts of association with any one, and not contributing the eighth. I clearly stated, from the beginning, that this grant of an eighth would end in nothing. It, however, belongs to me, the same as the third and the tenth, by virtue of the concession which Their Highnesses made in my favor. Out of the tenth I have got nothing, unless it is the tenth of what Their Highnesses themselves received. It must be, however, the tenth of all the gold and of everything found and obtained within the limits of my jurisdiction as Admiral, and of all the merchandise imported and exported into and from the said territory, after deducting the expenses. I have already explained that the reason of all this is set forth with clearness in the book of my privileges.

An effort must be made to obtain from Their Highnesses an answer to my letter and an order directing the people to be paid. I wrote on this subject four days ago, and sent the letter by Martin de Gamboa. You must have seen the letter which I sent to Juan Lopez at the same time as yours.

It is rumored here that the idea is entertained to create three or four bishoprics in the Indies, and the matter has been referred for study to the Bishop of Palencia. After presenting my compliments to that Bishop tell him that the service of Their Highnesses will be promoted if he wishes to confer with me on this subject before taking final action. Give my regards to Diego Mendez, and show him this letter. My illness prevents me from writing except at night. In the daytime my hands have no strength.

I think that a son of Francisco Pinelo will carry this letter. If so, receive him well, because he does for me with love and good will all that he can.

The caravel whose mast was broken when leaving Santo Domingo has arrived in the Algarves. She brings the record of the investigation in the Porres matter. So many ugly things and such a display of cruelty as will be shown there has never been seen. If Their Highnesses do not inflict proper punishment I do not know how any person will ever dare to go abroad and serve them, with people under his orders.

Today is Monday. I shall try to make your uncle and your brother leave here to-morrow. Remember that you must write very often to me, and tell Diego Mendez to write me a long letter. There are messengers who leave here every day for your place.

Our Lord may keep you in His holy guard. Done at Seville, December 1st, 1504.

Your father loves you as much as himself.

S.
S. A. S.
X. M. Y.
Xpo Ferens.

Facsimile of letter to Don Diego Columbus, December 3r l 1504.

XV.

LETTER FROM CHRISTOPHER COLUMBUS TO HIS SON DIEGO. DATED DECEMBER 3RD, 1504. ORIGINAL IN THE COLLECTION OF THE DUKE OF VERAGUA, MADRID.

†

My Dearest Son:

I wrote to you a long letter the day before yesterday and I sent it by Francisco Pinelo. Now, together with this letter I send to you a very full memorandum. I am astonished at not receiving any letter from you or the others, and this astonishment is shared by all those who are acquainted with me. Every one here has letters, but I, although more entitled than all to expect them, receive none. This is a matter about which more care ought to be taken. The memorandum to which I have referred explains itself, and for this reason I do not enter here into any details. Your brother, your uncle and Carbajal are going to join you, and through them you will learn what is not said here.

May Our Lord keep you in His holy guard.
Dated at Seville this 3rd of December, 1504.
Your father who loves you more than himself.

S.
S. A. S.
X. M. Y.
Xpo. Ferens.

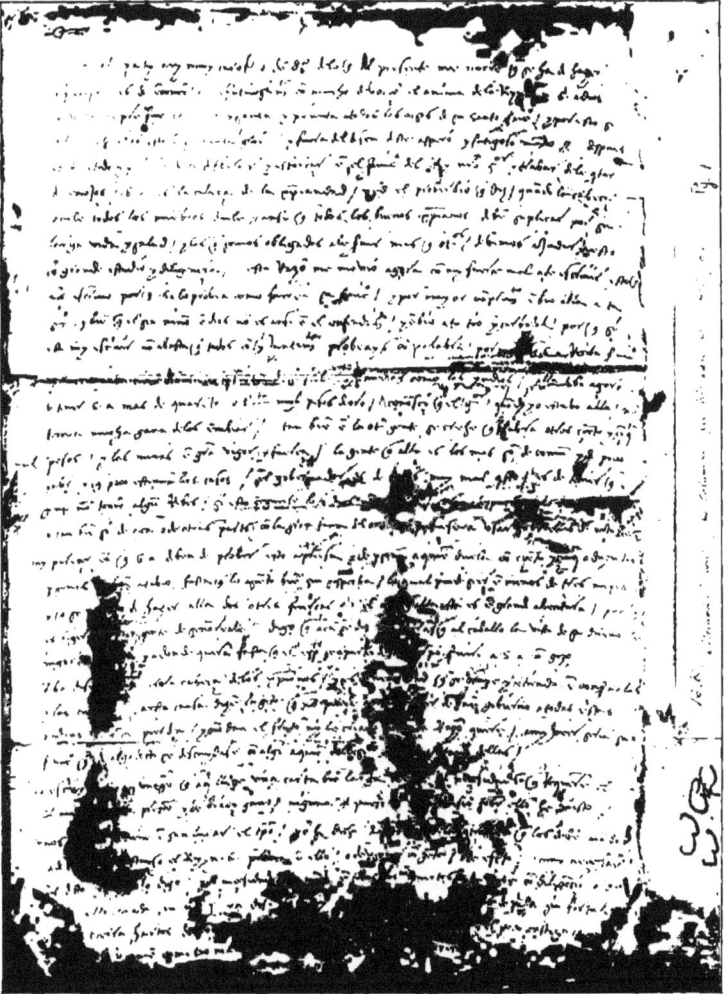

Facsimile of memorandum written to Don Diego Columbus, December 3rd, 1504.

XVI.

MEMORANDUM BY CHRISTOPHER COLUMBUS ENCLOSED TO HIS SON DIEGO IN LETTER DATED DECEMBER 3RD, 1504. ORIGINAL IN THE COLLECTION OF THE DUKE OF VERAGUA, MADRID.

Memorandum for you, my dearest son Don Diego, of what at present occurs to me must be done.

The principal thing is to commend to God, affectionately and with much devotion, the soul of the Queen, Our Lady. Her life was always catholic and holy. She was always ready for the things of God's holy service. And for this it must be believed that she is in His holy glory and beyond all desire relative to this rough and tiresome world.

Secondly, an effort should be made thoroughly and in all things to serve well the King, Our Lord, and prevent him from being displeased. His Highness is the head of all Christendom. Remember the proverb which says that when the head aches all the members ache also. Therefore all good Christians must pray for the preservation of his health, and for his being granted a long life; and those who, like ourselves, are bound to serve him more especially than others, must join the said prayers and do the said service with great care and diligence.

Whereupon, I have decided to write to you this memorandum, in spite of the great sufferings under which I am, in order that His Highness may be pleased to act as his own interest requires, and to make your efforts more efficient I have decided also to send your brother, who although a child in days is not a child in understanding, and also your uncle and Carbajal, so as to secure from you all together if my written words are not sufficient, such verbal representations as may be conducive to His Highness' service.

In my opinion there is nothing more in need of attention and remedy than the Indies. His Highness must have there at present more than 40,000 or 50,000 dollars in gold. I found out when I was there that the Governor had no desire to send that gold. It is believed among the people that an additional sum of 150,000 dollars must also be sent to His Highness. The mines continue to yield with steadiness and abundance. Most of the people there are extremely common and ignorant, who do not care much for anything. The Governor is unpopular with all of them, and it is to be feared that they may some

Facsimile of continuation of memorandum.

day do something wrong. If such a thing should happen, which God forbid, the remedy for the situation would be difficult. Neither would it be an easy thing to find redress for any trouble which might arise out of any injustice done either here or there, owing to the great fame of the gold. My opinion is that His Highness must attend to this at once, and entrust this business to a person who feels interest on the subject, and goes there with 150 or 200 persons, well prepared and equipped. That person must stay there until all matters are settled, and that cannot be done in less than three months. Provision must be made also to raise there two other forces, because, on account of the few people who can protect the gold kept there, it may easily disappear. There is a proverb which says that the eye of the owner makes the horse fat. Here and there and everywhere I shall serve with pleasure Their Highnesses as long as my soul remains united to my body.

I said before that His Highness is the head of Christendom, and that it is necessary for him to provide for the preservation of these lands. Some people say that he cannot, in the way that things go, provide the Indies with a good government and cause the same to yield the profits which reasonably must be expected. In my opinion, his entrusting this matter to some one who feels an interest in preventing ill-treatment of his subjects would prove favorable to his service.

I wrote to His Highness, as soon as I arrived here, and my letter which was very long, stated fully all the evils that require prompt and efficient remedy. I have received no answer, nor have I heard of any provision having been made on the subject.

Some vessels are detained at San Lucar on account of the weather. I have told the gentlemen of this Board of Trade (casa de contratacion) that they must detain them until they hear either by messenger or by letter of some disposition of the matter made by the King, Our Lord. This is a very necessary thing, and I know what I say. Orders must be sent to all the ports directing the authorities to be diligent in preventing people to go to the Indies without a permit. I have already said that a great deal is kept there in houses badly built and straw roofed, that there are many ruffians among the people; that everybody dislikes the Governor, and that no punishment has been or is inflicted upon those whodo wrong or prove thereby to be benefited. If His Highness decides to do something, it must be done quick, so as to cause no injury to the vessels.

I have heard that three Bishops are to be chosen to be sent to Hispaniola. If it pleases His Highness to hear me, before reaching a conclusion in this matter, I think that God, Our Lord, will be well served, and that His Highness will receive satisfaction.

P. S. I have explained at length what must be provided for the Hispaniola.

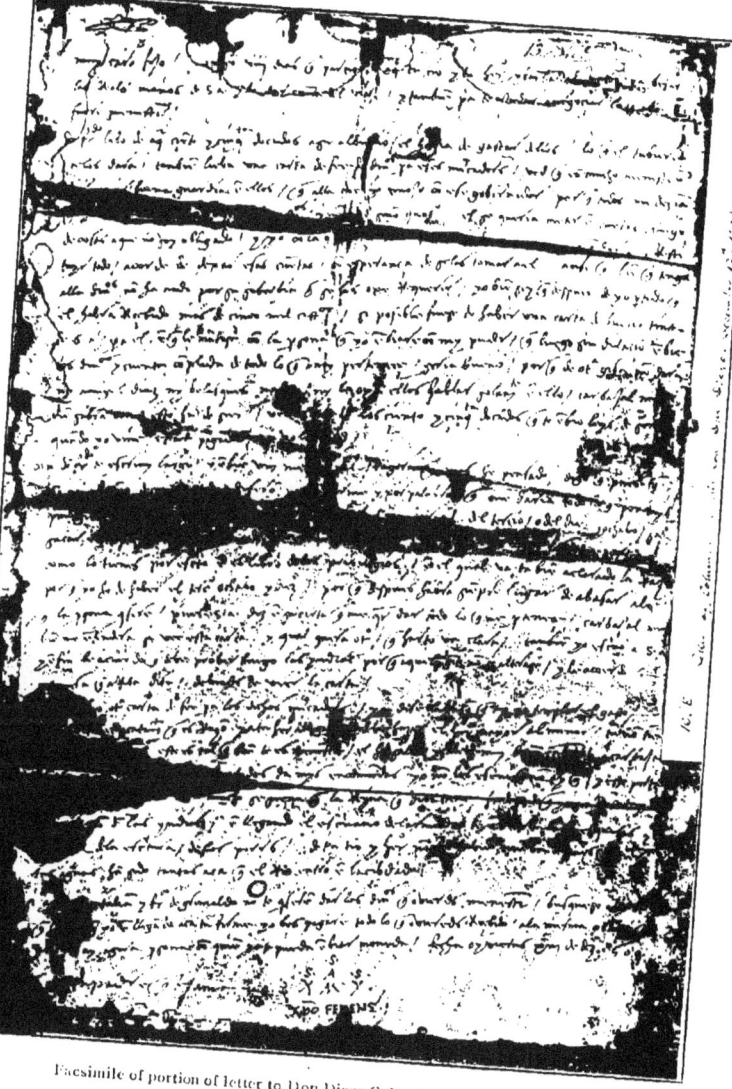

Facsimile of portion of letter to Don Diego Columbus, December 13th, 1504.

XVII.

LETTER FROM COLUMBUS TO HIS SON DIEGO. DATED DECEMBER 13TH, 1504. ORIGINAL IN THE COLLECTION OF THE DUKE OF VERAGUA, MADRID.

†

My Dearest Son:

Eight days have been completed to-day since the departure from here of your uncle, your brother and Carbajal, who went together to kiss the royal hands of His Highness and make a report of the voyage, and also to aid you in the negotiation of whatever may prove to be necessary.

Don Fernando left here with 150 ducats to be expended at his discretion. He will have to use some part of that money, but he will give you whatever he can. He also carries with him a letter of credit for some of your merchants there. You must be careful in this matter, because I have already had some trouble with your Governor, because everybody had told me that I had there some eleven or twelve thousand castellanos, and the result was that I had only four thousand. He wanted to charge me many things which I was not bound to pay, and I, trusting on the promises made by Their Highnesses that restitution of everything should be ordered to be made to me, decided to allow him to go on with his charges. I was in hopes that some day I could call him to account for that. He is so overbearing that nobody who has money there dares to ask for it.

I am well aware of the fact that after I left he received more than 5,000 castellanos; and if it were possible for you to obtain from His Highness a good letter to him, ordering him to deliver to whomever I may send with my power of attorney an account of what belongs to me and send the money, it would be very good for all,—otherwise he will give nothing. Miguel Diaz and Velazquez dare not even mention the subject to him. Carbajal knows very well how this can be fixed. Show him this letter. The 150 ducats which Luis Soria sent to you when I came have been paid as he wished.

I wrote you a long letter which I sent to you by Don Fernando. I also sent a memorandum. Now after having given further thoughts to the subject I shall say that whereas Their Highnesses stated verbally and also under their signature, at the time of my departure, that they would give me everything to which I am entitled under my letters of privilege, it is proper not to make any claim, either for the third, or the tenth or the eighth, mentioned in the memorandum, but to abide by the chapter of the letter in which their Highnesses told me what I have explained, and make the claim for all that belongs to me under my letters of privilege. You have the book in which all these grants have been copied, and you will find there the explanation of the reason why I had to have the third, and the tenth and the eighth. There will be always time to make reductions in the sum to be paid. But His Highness says in his letter that he wishes to give me all that belongs to me. Carbajal will understand all I mean, as soon as he reads this letter. Everyone else will also understand it, as the letter is plain enough.

I have also written to His Highness, and reminded him both of the necessity to take some measure in regard to the Indies to insure against some trouble among those people, and of the promises he made to me as above stated. It would be good for you to see this letter.

I send to you, now, another letter of credit for those merchants. I have explained the reason why the expenses must be moderate. Pay to your uncle that respect which is due to him, and treat you, brother as an elder brother must treat the younger. You have no other brother, and the Lord must be blessed for having made him such a good one. He has proved and continues to prove to be a person of very clear head. Honor Carbajal and Diego Mendez. Give my regards to them all, and tell them that I have not written to them because there is nothing to write, and the messenger, furthermore, is hurrying me up.

The rumor goes around in this place that the Queen, whom God has in his glory, left an order that I should be restored to the possession of the Indies.

As soon as the clerk of the fleet arrives here, I shall send to you the record of the investigation made, and the original writing to the Porres.

I have not heard from either your uncle or your brother, since they left here. The rains have been so heavy that the river overflowed, and entered the city.

If Agostin Italian and Francisco de Grimaldo are not willing to give you the money you may need, you must look for some others who may be willing to supply it. They must be sure that as soon as they send here your receipt, I shall honor your signature and pay at once all that was given to you. At present there is no person here with whom I might send the money to you.

Dated to-day, Friday, the 13th of December, 1504.
Your father who loves you more than himself.

S.
S. A. S.
X. M. Y.
Xpo Ferens.

XVIII.

LETTER OF CHRISTOPHER COLUMBUS TO HIS SON DIEGO, WRITTEN AT SEVILLE, DECEMBER 21ST, 1504. ORIGINAL IN COLLECTION OF THE DUKE OF VERAGUA, MADRID.

My Dearest Son:

The Adelantado and Carbajal and your brother left here for your place sixteen days ago, and I have not heard yet anything from them. Don Fernando took with him 150 ducats to attend to necessary expenses. He carried also a letter to the merchants ordering them to provide you with money. By Zamora, the postman, I sent you, afterwards, another of the same character, endorsed by Francisco de Rivarol, in which I told you not to use it if you had made use of the former one. Now, as I wish you not to lack money, I send you by Francisco Doria, but with the same injunction, a third letter of credit. I have already explained how necessary it is for us to be cautious in expending money until our affairs are settled by Their Highnesses. I also told you that in bringing these people to Castile I expended 1200 castellanos, most of which His Highness owes me. I wrote to His Highness on the subject, and asked for an order to settle that account.

I should like to have letters from you, if possible, every day. I complain of Diego Mendez and of Jerome for not writing to me, and also all the others, who as soon as they reach there, cease to correspond with me.

You must investigate whether the Queen, whom God has in His glory, said something in her will about me. It is also important for us to urge the Bishop of Palencia to hurry up. To him Their Highnesses are indebted for having the Indies—as he was the cause of my remaining in Castile, when I already had started to leave it. The Lord Chamberlain of His Highness must also be hurried up.

You must endeavor, when the opportunity arrives, that they see the instrument in writing which is in the book of my privileges, wherein the reason is explained, as I told you in another letter why the third, and the eighth, and the tenth are due to me.

I have written to my holy friend, the Father, because he complained of my silence. I send you a copy of this letter. I wish the King our Lord, or the Bishop of Palencia, would see this Father before I send my letter, so as to avoid misrepresentation. Camacho

Facsimile of portion of letter to Don Diego Columbus, from Seville, December 21st, 1504.

has made thousands of false statements against me. I would, much to my regret, arrest him. He is in the church, and says that when the holidays are over he will go there, if he can. He must prove what I owe him. I state upon my oath that I do not think I owe him anything, and that what he says is not true.

If without being importunate a permit can be obtained to ride on mule-back, I would try to go there after the month of January. But then I will start anyhow, in some other way, if the permit is not obtained. But let them make haste in providing the necessary for the preservation of the Indies and preventing their loss from being consummated.

May Our Lord keep you in His holy guard.
Dated December 21st.
Your father who loves you more than himself.

S.
S. A. S.
X. M. Y.
Xpo Ferens.

POSTSCRIPT TO LETTER XVIII. DATED DECEMBER 21ST, 1504.

This tenth which they give me is not the tenth promised. The letters of privilege explain it well. The tenth of the profit made out of all the merchandise brought here, and of all other things, is due to me — and nothing in this respect is given to me. Carbajal understands well what I mean. Carbajal must not forget to secure a letter from His Highness to the Governor directing him to send his accounts, at once, and without delay, and also all the moneys which I have there. And it would be better for us, as the said sum must be a large one, that His Highness should send one of his servants to receive it.

I will endeavor here to obtain from these Lords of the Board of Trade (contratacion) an order instructing the said Governor to send my money together with the gold belonging to Their Highnesses. But one thing must not interfere with the other. I think that the money belonging to me, accumulated there after my departure, amounts to seven or eight thousand dollars. Besides this, there is the money which they had retained before I left.

To my very dear son
Don Diego, at the
Court.

Facsimile of portion of letter to Nicolo Oderigo, December 27th, 1504.

XIX.

LETTER FROM COLUMBUS TO NICOLO ODERIGO, GENOESE AMBASSADOR TO SPAIN. FROM SEVILLE, DECEMBER 27TH, 1504. ORIGINAL IN THE MUNICIPAL PALACE, GENOA.

Virtuous Sir:

When I started on my voyage to the places from where I have just come, I spoke at length with you. I understand that you remember well all that then was said.

When returning here, I was in hopes to find some letters from you, or some messenger who would tell me verbally something in your name.

At about the same time of my departure from here, I sent to you by Francisco de Ribarol a book containing copies of several letters, and another in which all the grants and privileges given me were also copied, the whole inclosed in a red morocco case, with a silver lock. I also sent by the same man two letters for the St. George gentlemen, in which I assigned to them the tenth of my revenue, in consideration of and compensation for the reduction made on the duties on wheat and the other supplies. To nothing of this have I had any reply. Micer Francisco says that everything arrived safely. If this is the case, the failure of the St. George gentlemen to answer my letters is an act of discourtesy, for which the Treasury is by no means better off. This is the reason why it is generally said that to serve common people is serving no one.[1]

Another book of my privileges, equal (similar) to the one above mentioned, was left by me at Cadiz with Franco Catanio (who is the bearer of this letter), with instructions to send it to you,—in order that you should keep it together with the other, in some safe place, at your discretion.

At the time of my departure I received a letter from the King and Queen, my Lord and Lady. It is written there. Look at it, and you will find it very good. Nevertheless, Don Diego was not given possession, as it was promised.

While I was in the Indies I wrote to Their Highnesses, through three or four channels, about my voyage. One of those letters came back to me, and sealed as it was, I inclose it in this and send it to you. In another letter I inclose also a supplement to the above

---

[1] Quien sirve a comun, no sirve a ningun.

description of my voyage, and I pray you to give both to Micer Juan Luis, to whom I also have written and said that you will be the reader and interpreter of the said letters.

I am anxious to hear from you, especially about the plan which we agreed to.

I arrived here very sick, and at about the time which the Queen, my Lady (whom God has with him), died and I could not see her.

Up to the present, it is impossible for me to tell you what will be the practical result of all my doings. I suppose that Her Highness has properly provided in her will for everything concerning this matter, and the King, my Lord, always gives good answers.

Franco Catanio will verbally explain to you at length, all the rest.

May our Lord keep you in His guard.

From Seville, December 27th, 1504.

S.
S. A. S.
X. M. Y.
Xpo Ferens.
Great Admiral of the Ocean.
Viceroy and Governor General of the Indies.

XX.

LETTER FROM COLUMBUS TO HIS SON DIEGO. FROM SEVILLE, DECEMBER 29TH, 1504. ORIGINAL IN THE COLLECTION OF THE DUKE OF VERAGUA.

My Very Dear Son:

I wrote to you at great length, and sent my letter by Don Fernando who left here twenty-three days ago, in company with the Adelantado and Carbajal—and from none of you have I ever heard since. Sixteen days ago I wrote to you another letter, which I sent by Zamora, inclosing a letter of credit for the merchants there, endorsed by Francisco de Rivarol, ordering them to give you the money you might ask for. Subsequently, about eight days ago, I wrote to you again by another postman and inclosed another letter of credit, endorsed by Francisco Soria, and I addressed my communication in care of Pansaleon and Augustin, the Italians, who were requested to deliver it to you. I also inclosed a copy of a letter which I wrote to our holy friend the Father on the affairs of the Indies, to prevent him from complaining against me. And I sent this copy to you in order that either His Highness, or the Bishop of Palencia, may read it, and to avoid misrepresentations.

The pay of the people who went with me has been delayed; and I have had to provide for them as far as I could. They are poor, and moved by their anxiety to make a living decided to go there. They have been promised here to be dealt with as much favor as possible, and this is simply justice,—though there are some among them more deserving of punishment than of reward. I say this in reference to the runaways. I gave these people a letter for the Bishop of Palencia. Try to read it, and to cause your uncle, your brother, and Carbajal to read it also, so as to enable you all to aid the bearers in securing success for the petitions they are going to make to His Highness. You yourself must help them all that you can, as it is just, besides being a work of mercy. No people ever earned their money with so much danger and fatigue, as these have done,—and none other have rendered such a great service as they have. They say that Camacho and Master Bernal are anxious to go there. They are two of those creatures for whom God does not make many miracles. If they go, it will be to do harm rather than good. But they can do little, because truth shall always prevail, as it happened when so much turmoil was raised upon false statements at La Espanola. This Master Bernal was the one who started the treasonable movement. He was arrested, and charged with many crimes, for each

Facsimile of portion of letter to Don Diego Columbus, December 29th, 1504.

one of which he deserved to be quartered. At the request of your uncle and others he was pardoned, on condition however that said pardon would be revoked and he would be again liable to be punished in the proper way, if he would say the slightest thing against me and my officers. I inclose here a copy of the record which shows the whole of this business. As to Camacho, I will send you some legal papers referring to him. For more than eight days he has remained inside the church, without daring to leave it, for fear of the trouble into which he may get for his rashness and slanders. He has in his possession a will made by Terreros; but some relations of this Terreros have another will, subsequent in date, which annuls the former, as far as the disposition of the property is concerned. And I have been requested to attend to the fulfillment of the second will and the execution of all that is provided by it,—and therefore I am bound to compel Camacho to make restitution of what he has received. I shall attend to the preparation of the proper legal documents, which I shall have served on him. I believe that punishing him is a work of mercy. His tongue knows no restraint. Some one has to punish him, without the use of the rod, and that punishment will be harder for him and better for the conscience of the chastiser.

Diego Mendez is well acquainted with Master Bernal and his doings. The Governor wanted to put him in prison, while at La Espanola; but at my request he left him free. They say that he killed there two men, with some poison, in revenge for some wrong which did not amount to three beans.

If the permit to ride on mule-back can be obtained, without trouble, I would be pleased. Then I would like also to have a good mule.

Take advice with all about our business. Tell all others that do not write to them because of the great pains that writing makes me suffer. But they must not imitate my example, but on the contrary write to me, each one separately, and very often. How grieved I feel when I see that everybody here receives letters from there, and that I, who have so many of my people there, do not receive any. Give my regards to the Adelantado, to your brother and all the others.

Dated at Seville, December 29.

Your father who loves you more than himself.

S.
S. A. S.
X. M. Y.
Xpo Ferens.

I further say that if our affairs are to be settled according to the dictates of conscience, the chapter of the letter which Their Highnesses wrote to me, when I sailed, in which they said they would order to give you possession of all, must be shown and made use of. And then you must make use also of the instrument in writing in the book of my privileges, which explains the reason why in all justice and equity, the third, the eighth and the tenth are mine. There will be always time afterwards to make reductions.

Facsimile of portion of letter to Father Gaspar, January 4th, 1505.

XXI.

LETTER FROM COLUMBUS TO FATHER GASPAR CORRICIO, A CARTHUSIAN MONK AT THE MONASTERY OF LAS CUEVAS, NEAR SEVILLE. DATED JANUARY 4TH, 1505. ORIGINAL IN COLLECTION OF THE DUKE OF VERAGUA.

Reverend and Most Pious Father:

Diego Mendez has come from the Court. Don Diego is there well. The Adelantado and Don Fernando had not arrived yet. I will send them all to you with information of everything. I do not know how to say how much I wish to see you and communicate to you something which must not be trusted to the pen. I should like to peruse those instruments in writing and privileges which you have in your possession, and order a box to be made of cork, lined with wax, to keep those papers. I ask you as a great favor to send them all to me by that honest man, the lay brother, if he is coming, and if not, by Andrew, the brother of Juan Antonio, bearer of this letter.

I am, thanks to Our Lord, improving daily in my health.

My kind regards to the Reverend Father Superior, and to all the religious members of your house.

Dated this Saturday, the 4th of January.

Always ready to do what Your Reverence may command.

.S.
S. A. S.
X. M. Y.
Xpo Ferens.

XXII.

LETTER FROM COLUMBUS TO HIS SON DIEGO. DATED JANUARY 18TH, 1505. ORIGINAL IN THE COLLECTION OF THE DUKE OF VERAGUA, MADRID.

†

My Dearest Son:

I wrote to you a long letter which I forwarded by a messenger who will reach you to-day. I sent you also a letter for the Lord Chamberlain. I intended to inclose in it a copy of that chapter of the letter of Their Highnesses in which they promised to order you to be put in possession of everything; but I forgot to make the copy. Zamora, the postman, came. I read your letter, and also those of your uncle, your brother, and Carbajal. I was very happy to know that they had safely arrived, because I had experienced great anxiety in that respect. Diego Mendez will leave here, in three or four days, and will take the draft with him. He will carry also a full statement of everything. I shall write to Juan Velazquez, whose friendship and services I desire to obtain. I believe that he is a very honorable gentleman. Tell the Bishop of Palencia, if he has arrived there, or if not when he arrives, that I have been very much pleased with his prosperity, and that if I go there I will stop where he is, even if he is unwilling, and that we both have to come back to our first brotherly love for each other, which he will have no power to refuse, because my services to him will force him to grant it. The copy of my letter to our holy friend the Father was sent to you, as I said, in order that you might show it to the Bishop of Palencia, if he was there, or to the Archbishop of Seville, for fear that the King might have no time to look into this matter. I have told you that the petition to Their Highnesses must be for the fulfillment of what they wrote to me about the possession and of all the other promises which were then made; and I said that it was important to show him the chapter aforesaid of their letters. I recommended further that all of this should be done without delay, as it is advisable, for innumerable reasons, to act in this matter speedily. Let His Highness be persuaded that no matter how much he gives me it will be always in the proportion of one to one hundred when compared with the increase of his dominions and revenue, and furthermore, that what has been already done is nothing in comparison with what is to be done in the future. The sending of a Bishop to Hispaniola is a matter which must be delayed until I have spoken with His Highness, lest it may happen like in the other cases in which things were spoiled instead of being amended.

We have had here and still are having some very cold days—which have done and continue to do me much harm. Give my best regards to the Adelantado. May Our Lord bless you and your brother and keep you both in His holy guard. Remember me to Carbajal and Jerome. Diego Mendez will arrive there with his pocket full. I think that the business about which you wrote can be easily transacted. The vessels from the Indies have not yet arrived from Lisbon. They have brought much gold but none for me. Such a great mockery has never been seen. I left there sixty thousand dollars smelted. His Highness should not allow such great affairs to be ruined.

The Governor sends now some new application, but I do not know for what purpose. I am waiting for letters. Be careful in expending the money. It is advisable to do so.

Dated January 18th.

Your father who loves you more than himself.

S.
S. A. S.
X. M. Y.
Xpo Ferens.

Facsimile of portion of letter to Don Diego Columbus, February 5th, 1505.

XXIII.

LETTER FROM COLUMBUS TO HIS SON DIEGO. DATED FEBRUARY 5TH, 1505. ORIGINAL IN THE COLLECTION OF THE DUKE OF VERAGUA.

My Dearest Son:

Diego Mendez left here on Monday, the 3rd of the present month. After he left I spoke with Amerigo Vespusze, the bearer of this letter who goes there, where he has been called on business of navigation. He always wanted to please me. He is a very honest man. Fortune has been as adverse to him as to many others, and his labors have not been so profitable to him as it was reasonable to expect. He goes for my good, and very anxious to do everything which may prove beneficial to me if it is within his power. I do not know of any particular thing in which I might instruct him to my benefit, because I do not know exactly what he is wanted for there. But he goes determined to do for me all that he may possibly do. You must see what kind of service he may render to my advantage, and co-operate with him in having it rendered. He will work and speak and do everything suggested, but the suggestion must be made secretly so as to remove suspicion. I have told him all that can be said concerning these matters, and have informed him of the reward which they have given and continue to give to me.

This letter must be deemed as written also to the Adelantado, in order that he may see also what service Vespusze may render, and communicate with him.

His Highness must be sure that his vessels were in the best and richest part of the Indies, and if there is anything else to be known, in addition to what has been already said, I will give the information orally, because it is impossible to put it in writing.

May Our Lord keep you in His holy guard.

Dated at Seville, February 5th.

Your father who loves you more than himself.

S.
S. A. S.
X. M. Y.
Xpo Ferens.

XXIV.

LETTER FROM COLUMBUS TO HIS SON DIEGO, FEBRUARY 25TH, 1505.
ORIGINAL IN THE COLLECTION OF THE DUKE OF VERAGUA, MADRID.

My Dearest Son:

Licenciate De Zea is a gentleman to whom I want to do honor. He has in his charge the cases of two men who were subject to criminal prosecution, as it appears from the inclosed papers. See that Diego Mendez takes all the steps necessary to have those petitions presented to His Highness, together with the others, on the day of the coming Holy Week, in which it is customary to grant pardons. If the pardon is then granted, all right; but, if not, you all must look into some other manner of obtaining it.

May Our Lord keep you in His holy guard.

Dated at Seville, February 25th, 1505.

I wrote to you and sent the letter by Amerigo Vespusze. See that he sends to you the letter if you have not received it yet.

Your father,

Xpo Ferens.

XXV.

DRAFT OF LETTER OF COLUMBUS RELATING TO HIS CLAIMS AGAINST THE CROWN OF SPAIN, BASED UPON THE PRIVILEGES AND CONCESSIONS GRANTED TO HIM BY THE CONTRACT WITH THE SPANISH SOVEREIGNS, FERDINAND AND ISABELLA. ORIGINAL IN THE COLLECTION OF THE DUKE OF BERWICK-ALBA, MADRID.

"Report on my privileges and concessions.
Jhs cumas, t no . . ."
Jesus cum Mari sit nobis in vita
(May Jesus and Mary be with us in life).

MAGNIFICENT SIRS:

It appears from your privilege and the articles of agreement entered into with you, that their Highnesses appointed you Admiral of the Ocean Seas, which they defined by causing a line to be drawn from pole to pole, crossing the Cape Verde Islands and the Azores, and that they granted to you exactly the same rights, honors, and favors as are enjoyed by the Lord Admiral of Castile within his own district.

Item. They graciously appointed you also Viceroy and Governor-General of all the islands and continents, whether already discovered or to be discovered, on the other side of the line aforesaid, and they granted you the power to appoint all the officers who should be required for the administration of the government of the said islands and continents.

Item. They also gave you the tenth of everything received from the district subject to your jurisdiction as Admiral, after deducting the expenses.

Item. They gave you, likewise, the eighth of all the profits made out of expeditions, or fleets sent to the Indies, to the equipment of which you had contributed by paying one-eighth of the expenses.

It appears from the acts of confirmation of your privileges that you are the discoverer of the islands and continents of the Indies. If anything is now discovered there, it will be owing to you and your industry, and can not properly be called discovery. You are the one who discovered the Indies, in spite of the doubts which were raised about their existence, and of the great opposition raised against you both by men of learning and by people of practical knowledge in navigation and matters connected with the sea, who all said that you were joking and that God had never placed any land where you said. Whoever goes now to the Indies, even if he goes to places where you never set your foot, cannot, as against you, be called a discoverer, for he only goes to a district which is already under your jurisdiction as admiral, and enters seas or lands which were discovered by you. Under these circumstances, your rights and authority as Admiral and Viceroy and Governor-General, and your power to make appointments for all offices are to be exercised in and over the whole district, whether on land or on the sea, whether already traveled or to be traveled hereafter, on the other side of the line which has been mentioned before. Beyond that line you are the only one having authority to attend in the name of their Highnesses to all the business of the Government, to hear and decide all cases and causes, to affix the Royal Seal entrusted to you for such purposes, to all letters patent to be issued there, to administer justice in civil and criminal matters, and to have and exercise full power and jurisdiction in everything relative to the administration of said Government, as more in full described in the ordinances and letters of concession and privileges which I have examined.

It appears, furthermore, that by a Royal letter of 1497, issued at Medina, their Highnesses freed you from sharing the expenses incurred up to that date on account of this business, and exempted you also from contributing toward defraying the expenses of the expedition which was then being equipped and you had to take to the Indies. The said Royal letter says that you are bound to pay nothing on this account, except in case of expenses incurred subsequent to your arrival at Hispaniola. You are free from paying expenses prior to that moment; but you cannot, either, demand anything out of what was brought here during the same period.

As you admit to having arrived there on the 31st of August, 1489, a liquidation must be made of all the expenses incurred ever since, and you shall be bound to contribute such portion thereof as has been agreed upon.

From the agreements entered into with the Lord Admiral of Castile, it appears that he is entitled to one-third of all the profits made on the sea, either by him or their Highness' navy. Whereupon, under your own letters of concession, which gave you exactly the same rights and privileges as are given the Lord Admiral of Castile, you are entitled to a third of the profits.

It appears from the agreements entered into with you, in regard to the share you ought to have out of the profits made and to be made in this business of the Indies, that the said share belongs to you under three different considerations and for three different reasons. Your share under each head is clearly stated, and there is no possibility of error or misunderstanding in this respect. The liquidation of the profits is simply a matter of arithmetic, as in the following example:

A man fits out a vessel and says to one of his servants: I make you master of this vessel; go, and you shall have one-third of all the profits. Then he calls another servant and says to him: Go on board the vessel to be the purser and you shall have the tenth. Finally he calls a third servant and tells him: Go as a clerk, and whereas you have contributed one-eighth of the expenses you shall have also the eighth part of the profits.

The vessel sailed, and on her return it was found out that the profits amounted to ten ducats. The master says then to the man who fitted out the vessel: "Sir, the profits amount to ten ducats, order the third part of that sum to be given to me as promised," and so he ordered. Then comes the purser and says: "Sir, the profits were ten ducats; order a tenth of that sum to be given to me as promised," and so he ordered. Finally the clerk comes and says: "Sir, I contributed one-eighth of the expenses to fit out this vessel; the profits made by her are ten ducats, cause one-eighth of these ten ducats to be given to me," and so he did.

An account like this is to be made to liquidate the share which, under the concessions made in your favor in this business of the Indies, belongs to you. It would be wrong to give you the tenth of the whole, and then the eighth of the balance, not of the whole, and then the third of the second balance, and not also of the whole. Such a manner of making the calculation would be unacceptable, as each chapter of heading clearly fixes the portion which under it must be paid to you.

In regard to the expenses my opinion is that as our Lord has given enough in this business to pay amply all those which have been incurred, you might as well be satisfied with seeing them paid, if so pleases their Highnesses, out of the gold or anything else of value which may be found there, and with having your share of the profits paid to you by their Highnesses out of the net balance.

I have noticed that your deeds contain a provision, made by their Highnesses, ordering that nothing must be done in regard to the Indies without your personal intervention or the intervention of a person having your power of attorney.

I have also noticed another provision under which nothing can be sent to the Indies without your signature and the signature of the person appointed at Cadiz for such purposes by their Highnesses, nor can anything brought from the Indies be received here without the signature both of the said person and of the deputy comptroller.

I have seen also a bull of the Holy Father which is on file among your papers, which states that you were and are the one who discovered and won those Indies as a servant of their Highnesses.

From all your letters of privileges and concessions it appears, as already stated, that you must have by reason of your rights, equal to those of the Lord Admiral of Castile, one-third of everything obtained within the limits placed under your jurisdiction as Admiral of the Ocean Sea, and by reason of your other concessions the eighth and the tenth of the same. If their Highnesses make some other concessions in the Indies without saying what is yours a wrong will be inflicted upon you, and this wrong will be done whether the new concession applies to money matters or in regard to the right of making appointments, or whether it concerns so-called new discoveries or not. The discovery of the Indies was, as above stated, the basis and the consideration upon which the agreements were made and entered into with you and executed and signed, and as soon as you discovered the first island you discovered the Indies, and your part of the contract was fulfilled. It was then that the Indies were given to their Highnesses by the bull of donation issued by the Pope.

Their Highnesses are in conscience bound to indemnify you for all damages which, and deprivation of your rights, may cause you to sustain.

Gentlemen, I ask for nothing, and I place into the Royal hands of the Queen and refer to her all that is stated in the foregoing writing. I shall show to your lordships my titles and letters of privilege whenever desired.

Another privilege which I have seen in your papers granted to you is the power to convey your office of Viceroy and Admiral and Governor-General and all your property unto Don Diego, your son, or unto whomsoever you may be pleased, and that none of the said offices and nothing of the said property can ever be taken away, whether for debts or criminal offense, unless the latter is a crime lessæ majestatis.

(See frontispiece for fac-simile of No. XXVI on next page.)

XXVI.

AUTOGRAPHIC STATEMENT BY COLUMBUS OF GOLD BROUGHT FROM AMERICA AND SOLD BY HIM IN CASTILE. DATE UNKNOWN. PROBABLY IN 1493. ORIGINAL IN THE COLLECTION OF THE DUKE OF BERWICK-ALBA, MADRID.

On July 13 Christobal de Torres sold at Seville 2 marks, 7 ounces, 4 ochavas of gold, at 453, the weight of a castellano.

On August 12, at Valladolid, Carbajal sold 2 marks, 6 ounces, 4 ochaves, 3 tomins, almost all of which was given by him in payment of the clothing which he bought for himself.

September 11, at Arcos, Carbajal sold 6 ounces, 2 ochaves, 1 tomin, 3 grains. All was sold at ....

September 19, Burgos, 4 ounces, 7 ochaves, 3 tomins were weighed.

October 7, Carbajal sold 7 ounces, 4 ochaves, 5 tomins, 3 grains, at 445.

October 25, Burgos, Carbajal sold 7 ounces, 4 ochaves, 5 tomins, 3 grains, at 445.

November 12, 4 Burgos, Carbajal sold 1 mark, 6 ounces and 7 ochaves, less 14 grains, at 438.

December 17, Burgos, Carbajal sold 7 ounces, 2 ochaves and 3 tomins, at 446.

January 10, Burgos, Carbajal sold 1 mark, 6 ounces, 1 ochave, at.......

February 6, Burgos, Carbajal sold 7 ounces, 4 ochaves, 4 tomins, 4 grains, at 445.

February 13, Burgos, Juan Antonio sold 7 ounces, 6 ochaves, 1 tomin, at 450.

February 28, Burgos, Juan Antonio sold 4 marks, 5 ounces, 6 ochaves and 3 tomins, at 450.

March 15, or before, Burgos, Juan Antonio sold 1 mark, (this item covers the transaction or business of the "funda") charged to him at 453.

December 30, Burgos, Juan Antonio sold to the silversmith who made the seal 4 ounces, 2 ochaves, 3 tomins, at 448.

January 24, Burgos, Carbajal sold 1 mark, 4 ochaves, 3 tomins, at ....

March 3, Juan Antonio gave to the silversmith in payment of the necklace made by him, 1 ounce and 2 tomins, at 453.

The sum of 91 reals was due to the said silversmith for 47 links, which the necklace has, at 2 reals per link.

At the foot of the page, on the left corner, Columbus made the following note: "Two hundred and thirty-four doredos which Don Diego gave me on ...."

The title given by Columbus to this paper, written by him across the left margin, was; "Statement of the gold sold in Castile up to the months of ...."

XXVII.

TRANSLATION OF ORIGINAL DRAFT BY COLUMBUS FOR ONE HUNDRED GOLD CASTELLANOS. DATED AT GRANADA, OCTOBER 22ND, 1501. ORIGINAL IN THE COLLECTION OF THE DUKE OF BERWICK-ALBA, MADRID.

†

Most Virtuous Sir:

I pray you to cause one hundred gold castellanos, which I need here to go to Seville to be loaned to me. You will be pleased to order them to be given to the bearer, Diego Tristan, my Majordomo, who will acknowledge the receipt thereof on the back of this draft.

Done on Friday, the 22nd of October, 1501.

S.
S. A. S.
X. M. Y.
The Admiral.

On the back. (In the handwriting of some one else).

The Admiral of the Indies. 3 x 1 v ii j p d.

I, Diego Tristan, do hereby acknowledge to have received of the treasurer, Alonzo de Morales, the one hundred castellanos to which the present draft of the Admiral refers, said amount being equal to 48,500 maravedis. In testimony of which I have hereunto subscribed my name, at Granada, on the 23rd of October, 1501.

Diego Tristan. (Autograph).

Memorandum in continuation of the above in Columbus' handwriting:

The above amount was deducted from the 150,000 which afterward were given to me at Seville, by order of Her Highness, to aid me in defraying the expenses, and the receipt of which I acknowledged.

XXVIII.

TRANSLATION OF THE CONTRACT BETWEEN COLUMBUS AND THE SOVEREIGNS. FIRST VOYAGE. ORIGINAL IN THE COLLECTION OF THE DUKE OF VERAGUA, MADRID.

In the name of the Holy Trinity and Eternal Unity, Father, Son and Holy Ghost, three persons really distinct and one divine essence, who lives and reigns forever without end; and of the most Blessed Virgin, glorious Holy Mary, our Lady, His Mother, whom we hold as Lady and Advocate in all our undertakings; and to the honor and reverence of her, and of the most blessed Apostle St. James, light and mirror of the Spains, patron and guide of the Kings of Castile and of Leon; and likewise to the honor and reverence of all the other Saints of the Celestial Court; as man, by whatever knowledge he mat have of the world, cannot, according to nature, completely know what God is, but may know Him by seeing and contemplating His wonders and the works and deeds which He performed and performs every day, because all the works are the effect of His power and are governed by his wisdom and maintained by His goodness; and so, man may understand that God is the beginning, the middle and the end of all things; and that they are included in Him and He maintains each one in that state in which He placed it in the order (of the world), and all stand in need of Him and He of none, and He can change them whenever it may be agreeable to His will, and He can not be subjected to change, nor be changed in anything; and He is called the King of Kings, because from Him they derive their name and reign through Him, and He governs and preserves them, who are Vicars (each one in His own kingdom), placed by Him over the people to maintain them temporarily in justice and in truth, which is fully demonstrated in two ways—the one spiritual, according as the prophets and saints demonstrated, upon whom our Lord conferred the grace of understanding those things certainly and made them to be understood by others; the other natural, as the philosophers demonstrated, who understood those things naturally, for the saints declared that the King is established upon earth in the place of God to render justice and give to every one his right, and on this account they called him the heart and soul of the people; and as the soul resides in the heart of man and the body lives and is preserved by it, so justice is established in the King, which is the life and preservation of the people of his dominions. And as the heart is one, and through it all the other members receive unity so as to form one body, in like manner all the inhabitants of the kingdom, although many, are one, because the King must be and is one, and through him all have to be one with him to follow and assist him in the things he has to perform. Then philosophers naturally declared that Kings are the head of kingdoms, for in the same manner as sentiment springs from the head, which commands all the other members of the body, in like manner by the command which emanates from the King, Lord and Head of all, the inhabitants of the kingdom must be directed and governed, and that they have to obey him; and so great is the right of kingly power that all the laws and rights are in the power of Kings, who acknowledge it not from men, but from God, whose place they hold in temporal affairs. Among other things it especially behooves the King to love, honor and preserve his people, and among these things he must particularly distinguish and honor persons meritorious, either by services rendered to him or on account of their being endowed with goodness. And as, according to the sayings of the wise, justice is one of the virtues peculiar to kings, which is the support and truth of things, by which the world is better and more justly preserved, being likewise a fountain from which every right is derived and remains always alive in the minds of just men and never fails, giving and distributing to each one equally his right, and embracing in itself all the principal virtues; and very great utility arises from it, because it engages every person to live with prudence and in peace according to his state without fault and without error, the good becoming through it better by receiving a reward for their deeds rightly performed, and the others correcting themselves and entering through it into the right road. Of which justice there are two principal parts—the one is communicative between man and man, the other is distributive, which carries with it the rewards and recompenses of the good and virtuous labor; and services which individuals render to Kings and Princes and to the commonweal of their kingdoms; and as the conferring a reward upon those who serve well and faithfully is an attribute, as the law says, very becoming to all mankind, and more especially to kings,

Princes and great Lords, who have the power of doing it, and whose proper office it is to honor and elevate those who serve them well and faithfully and who are worthy of it on account of their virtues and services; and kings in conferring rewards upon worthy actions show by that their acknowledgement of virtue and love of justice, for justice consists not only in giving an example of punishment as a terror to the wicked, but likewise in recompensing the good, and besides this a signal advantage arises from it, because it excites the good to become better and the wicked to correct themselves, and by not acting thus the contrary might take place, and since among other rewards, and remunerations which Kings have in their power to bestow upon them truly-and faithfully, there is that of honoring and elevating them above all the others of their race and ennobling, decorating and honoring them, and conferring many other kindnesses, favors and graces upon them.

We, considering and reflecting upon the above said things, will, that, by this our patent of privilege, and by a copy of it signed by a public scrivener, present and future generations may know, that, We, Don Ferdinand and Dona Isabella, by the grace of God, King and Queen of Castile, Leon, Aragon, Sicily, Granada, Toledo, Valencia, Galacia, Majorca, Seville, Sardinia, Corsica, Murcia, Jahen, Algarve, Algesira, Gibraltar, and the Canary Islands, Count and Countess of Barcelona, Lords of Biscay and Molina, Dukes of Athens and Neopatria, Counts of Roussillon and Cerdan, Marquises of Orestan and Goziano, have seen a patent of grace signed with our names, and sealed with our seal, drawn up as follows:

Don Ferdinand and Dona Isabella, by the grace of God, King and Queen of Castile, Leon, Aragon, Sicily, Granada, Toledo, Valencia, Galacia, Majorca, Seville, Sardinia, Cordova, Corsica, Murcia, Jahen, Algarve, Algesira, Gibraltar, and the Canary Islands, Count and Countess of Barcelona, Lords of Biscay and Molina, Dukes of Athens and Neopatria, Counts of Roussillon and Cerdan, Marquises of Orestan and Goziano: Inasmuch as you, Christopher Columbus, are going by our commands to discover and conquer, with some of our vessels and our subjects, certain islands and mainland in the ocean, and as it is hoped, with the assistance of God, that some of the aforesaid islands and mainland in the said ocean will be discovered and conquered through your labor and industry; and it being just and reasonable that for exposing yourself to such danger for our service, you should be rewarded: We, desiring on that account to do you honor and favor, declare it to be our will and pleasure, that you, the above said Christopher Columbus, when you shall have discovered and conquered the said islands and mainland in the said ocean, or any one whatsoever of them, be our Admiral of the said islands and mainland, which you shall thus discover and conquer, and be our Admiral, Viceroy and Governor of them and that you may, from this time forward, style and entitle yourself Don Christopher Columbus; and likewise your children and successors in the said office and charge, may entitle and call themselves, Don, Admiral, Viceroy and Governor of them; and that you may use and exercise the said office of Admiral, with the aforesaid office of Viceroy and Governor of the above said islands and mainland, which you discover and conquer, by yourself as well by means of your lieutenants, and hear and determine all suits, and civil and criminal causes respecting the said office of Admiral, and of Viceroy and Governor, according as you will find by right, and in the manner in which the Admirals of our kingdoms were accustomed to use and exercise it; and that you may punish and chastise delinquents; and use the said office of Admiral, Viceroy and Governor, you and your above said lieutenants, in all that concerns and is annexed to the said offices, and to each one of them; and that you may have and receive the rights and fees belonging and annexed to the said offices and to each of them; according as our high admiral in the admirality of our kingdoms receives, and is accustomed to receive them. And by this our patent, or by a copy of it, signed by a public scrivener, we command the Prince Don John, our most dearly beloved son, the Infantes, dukes, prelates, marquises, counts, masters of orders, priors, companions, and those of our council; and the auditors of our chamber, alcaldes, and other officers of justice, whoever they may be, of our household, court and Chancery, and the governors of castles and strong and open places; and all counselors, assistants, corregidors, alcaldes, bailiffs and sheriffs, and the twenty-four sworn chancellors, esquires, officers, and good men of all the cities, towns and places of our kingdoms and dominions, and of those which you shall conquer and acquire, and the captains, masters, mates and officers, mariners and seamen, our subjects and natives, who now are and shall be hereafter, and every one, and whomsoever of them; that the said islands and mainland in the ocean, being discovered and acquired by you, and they being taken, and the solemnities that are required on such occasions having been observed by you, or by the person who shall receive the power for you, to have and to hold to you hereafter, during all your life, and after you, your son and successor, and from successor to successor forever, as our Admiral of the said ocean, and as Viceroy and Governor of the aforesaid islands and mainland, which you, the above said Don Christopher Columbus, shall discover and acquire; and to treat of whatever regards such things with you, and with your above said lieutenants, whom you shall place in the said offices of Admiral, Viceroy and Governor, and to exact and cause to be exacted for you, with quittance, the fees and other things annexed and belonging to the said officers, and to observe, and cause to be observed towards you all the honors, graces, favors, liberties, pre-eminences, prerogatives, exemptions and immunities, and all and every other thing which by right of the said offices of Admiral, Viceroy and Governor you are to have and enjoy, and which are to be maintained to you in all, well and completely, in such manner as not to be diminished in anything, and not place, nor permit to be placed, any sequestration upon, nor offer any opposition to them; because, We, with this our patent, now and forever, make a grant to you of the said offices of Admiral, Viceroy and Governor, by right of inheritance forever; and we give you possession of them, and of every one of them, with the power and authority to use and exercise them, and to take the fees and salaries annexed and belonging to them, and every one of them according as has been said. As for such as has been said, if it were necessary, and if you should demand it, we order our chancellor, notaries, and other officers who are employed in the office of our seals, to give, expediate and seal for you, our patent to privilege, folded up in the form of a roll; in the strongest, most firm, and fit manner, and that you may demand of them, what may be necessary for you; and none of you act, nor let act otherwise in any manner, under the penalty of our displeasure, and of ten thousand maravedis for our chamber, upon any pretense whatsoever. And moreover, we enjoin the individual, who presents to you this our patent, to cite you to appear before our presence in our courts, wherever we may be, within the fifteen days next following the day of the citation, under the aforesaid penalty; under which we command every public scrivener whatsoever, who for this purpose shall be called upon, to give to him who shall have presented this paper a certificate signed with his signet, in order that he may know how our command is executed.

Given in our city of Granada, on the thirteenth day of the month of April, in the year of the nativity of our Lord Jesus Christ, one thousand four hundred and ninety-two.

I, THE KING.
I, THE QUEEN.

XXIX.

ROYAL LETTERS PATENT FROM THE SOVEREIGNS OF SPAIN, COMMANDING THE INHABITANTS OF PALOS TO FURNISH CHRISTOPHER COLUMBUS EVERYTHING NECESSARY TO EQUIP THE CARAVELS FOR HIS FIRST VOYAGE. ORIGINAL IN THE COLLECTION OF THE DUKE OF VERAGUA, MADRID.

Don Ferdinand and Dona Isabella, by the grace of God, King and Queen of Castile, Leon, Aragon, etc., etc., to you Diego Rodriguez Prieto, and to all other persons inhabitants of the town of Palos. Greeting: You are well aware that in consequence of some offense which we received at your hands, you were condemned by our council to render us the service of two caravels armed at your own expense for the space of twelve months whenever and wherever it should be our pleasure to demand the same, this service to be rendered under certain penalties as stated more at large in the sentence given against you.

And, inasmuch as we have ordered Christopher Columbus to proceed with a fleet of three caravels, as our captain, to certain parts of the ocean, upon a matter connected with our service, and we desire that the two caravels, the service of which you owe us as above said, should be placed at his disposal—we hereby order that within ten days from the sight of this letter, without delay or waiting for any further directions, you have in complete readiness the said two armed caravels for the service of the above said Christopher Columbus in the enterprise upon which we have dispatched him, and that they be placed at his command from that time forth; and for the crews of the said two caravels we order him to pay you forthwith four months' wages at the same rate with which the crew of the other caravel is paid, being the common allowance for ships of war.

The vessels thus placed under his direction shall follow the route ordered by him on our part, and obey him in all other orders, provided that neither you nor the said Christopher Columbus, nor any other person belonging to the said caravels, shall proceed to the mine nor to the countries in that neighborhood occupied by the King of Portugal, our brother, as it is our desire to adhere to the agreement existing between us and the said King of Portugal upon that head.

And having received a certificate from the said captain that he had received the said two caravels from you, and is satisfied with the same, we shall consider you as having discharged the obligation imposed upon you by our council as above said, and we hereby declare you henceforth free from the same; but in the event of the non-fulfillment of or procrastination of the above order, we shall forthwith command the execution of the penalties contained in the aforesaid sentence, upon each one of you and your goods.

The above requisition is to be complied with throughout, under pain of our displeasure and a penalty of ten thousand maravedis for the non-performance of any part thereof, to which end we hereby order under the said penalty, whatever public notary may be called upon for that purpose to furnish you with the proper signed attestations, that we may be assured of the fulfillment of our orders.

I, THE KING.
I, THE QUEEN.

Given in the City of Granada, on the thirtieth day of April, in the year of Our Lord Jesus Christ one thousand four hundred and ninety-two.

JUAN DE COLOMA,
Secretary of the King and Queen, etc.

Done in due form,
RODERICUS, Doctor.
Registered,
SEBASTIAN DE OLANO,
FRANCISCO DE MADRID,
Chancellor.

XXX.

ROYAL LETTERS PATENT FROM THE SOVEREIGNS OF SPAIN GRANTING LICENSE TO THE PERSONS ACCOMPANYING COLUMBUS ON HIS FIRST VOYAGE. ORIGINAL IN THE COLLECTION OF THE DUKE OF VERAGUA, MADRID.

Don Ferdinand and Dona Isabella, by the grace of God, King and Queen of Castile, Leon, Aragon, etc., etc. To the members of our Council, Oidors of our Court of Audience, Corregidores, Asistentes, Alcades, Alguaeils, Merinos, and all other magistrates whatsoever of all the cities, towns and villages of our kingdoms and dominions, to every one who shall see this writing or a copy of the same attested by a public notary, Greeting:

Be it known to you that we have ordered Christopher Columbus to proceed to sea for the accomplishment of certain business for our service, and as we are informed by him that in order to man the fleet which he is to command for the execution of this purpose, it is necessary to grant security to the persons composing the crew of the same, who would be otherwise unwilling to embark, and being requested by him to give the necessary orders for this measure, we have determined to grant what is demanded by him relating to this matter.

We therefore grant a security to each and every person belonging to the crews of the fleet of the said Christopher Columbus, in the voyage by sea which he is to undertake by our command, exempting them from all hindrance or inconvenience either in their persons or goods; and we declare them privileged from arrest or detention on account of any offense or crime which may have been committed by them up to the date of this instrument, and during the time they may be upon the voyage, and for two months after they return to their homes.

And we hereby command you, all and each one, in your several districts and jurisdictions, that you abstain from trying any criminal cause touching the person of the crews under the command of the said Christopher Columbus, during the time above specified, it being our will and pleasure that every matter of this sort remain suspended. This order is to be complied with as you value our favor, and under a penalty of ten thousand maravedis for any infringement of the same.

And we hereby furthermore command every public notary who shall be applied to for any purpose connected with the above mentioned mandate, that he furnish all the proper signed attestations which are necessary in the case, in order that we may be assured of the due performance of our orders.

I, THE KING.
I, THE QUEEN.

> Given in our City of Granada, on the thirtieth day of April, in the year of Our Saviour Jesus Christ, one thousand four hundred and ninety-two

JUAN DE COLOMA,
Secretary.

Executed in due form,
RODERICUS, Doctor.
FRANCISCO DE MADRID,
Chancellor.

XXXI.

LETTER OF COLUMBUS TO LOUIS SANTANGEL, GIVING AN ACCOUNT OF HIS FIRST VOYAGE AND THE DISCOVERY OF THE NEW WORLD. SENT OVERLAND FROM LISBON, FEBRUARY, 1493, AND PUBLISHED IN MARCH, 1493. ORIGINAL PROBABLY DESTROYED BY PRINTER.

Sir: As I am sure you will be pleased at the great victory which the Lord has given me in my voyage I write this to inform you that in twenty days I arrived in the Indies with the squadron which their Majesties had placed under my command. There I discovered many islands, inhabited by a numerous population, and took possession of them for their Highnesses, with public ceremony and the royal flag displayed, without molestation.

The first that I discovered I named San Salvador, in remembrance of that Almighty Power which had so miraculously bestowed them. The Indians call it Guanahani. To the second I assigned the name of Santa Marie de Conception; to the third that of Fernandina; to the fourth that of Isabella; to the fifth Juana; and so on, to every one a new name.

When I arrived at Juana, I followed the coast to the westward and found it so extensive that I considered it must be a continent and a province of Cathay. And as I found no towns or villages by the seaside, excepting some small settlements, with the people of which I could not communicate because they all ran away, I continued my course to the westward, thinking I should not fail to find some large town and cities. After having coasted many leagues without finding any signs of them, and seeing that the coast took me to the northward, where I did not wish to go, as the winter was already set in, I considered it best to follow the coast to the south; and the wind being also scant, I determined to lose no more time, and therefore returned to a certain port, from whence I sent two messengers into the country to ascertain whether there was any king there or any large city.

They traveled for three days, finding an infinite number of small settlements and an innumerable population, but nothing like a city: on which account they returned. I had tolerably well ascertained from some Indians whom I had taken that this land was only an island, so I followed the coast of it to the east 107 leagues, to its termination. And about eighteen leagues from this cape, to the east, there was another island, to which I shortly gave the name of Espanola. I went to it, and followed the north coast of it, as I had done that of Juana, for 178 long leagues due east.

This island is very fertile, as well, indeed, as all the rest. It possesses numerous harbors, far superior to any I know in Europe, and what is remarkable, plenty of large inlets. The land is high, and contains many lofty ridges and some very high mountains, without comparison of the Island of Centrefrey; all of them very handsome and of different forms; all of them accessible and abounding in trees of a thousand kinds, high, and appearing as if they would reach the skies. And I am assured that the latter never lose their fresh foliage, as far as I can understand, for I saw them as fresh and flourishing as those of Spain in the month of May. Some were in blossom, some bearing fruit, and others in other states, according to their nature.

The nightingale and a thousand kinds of birds enliven the woods with their song, in the month of November, wherever I went. There are seven or eight kinds of palms, of various elegant forms, besides various other trees, fruits and herbs. The pines of this island are magnificent. It has also extensive plains, honey, and a great variety of birds and fruits. It has many metal mines, and a population innumerable.

Española is a wonderful island, with mountains, groves, plains, and the country generally beautiful and rich for planting and sowing, for rearing sheep and cattle of all kinds, and ready for towns and cities. The harbors must be seen to be appreciated; rivers are plentiful and large and of excellent water; the greater part of them contain gold. There is a great difference between the trees, fruits and herbs of this island and those of Juana. In this island there are many spices, and large mines of gold and other metals.

The people of this island and of all the others which I have discovered or heard of, both men and women, go naked as they were born, although some of the women wear leaves of herbs or a cotton covering made on purpose. They have no iron or steel, nor any weapons; not that they are not a well-disposed people and of fine stature, but they are timid to a degree. They have no other arms excepting spears made of cane, to which they fix at the end a sharp piece of wood, and then dare not use even these. Frequently I had occasion to send two or three of my men on shore to some settlement for information, where there would be multitudes of them; and as soon as they saw our people they would run away every soul, the father leaving his child; and this was not because any one had done them harm, for rather at every cape where I had landed and been able to communicate with them I have made them presents of cloth and many other things without receiving anything in return; but because they are so timid. Certainly, where they have confidence and forget their fears they are so open-hearted and liberal with all they possess that it is scarcely to be believed without seeing it. If anything that they have is asked of them they never deny it; on the contrary, they will offer it. Their generosity is so great that they would give anything, whether it is costly or not, for anything of every kind that is offered them and be contented with it. I was obliged to prevent such worthless things being given them as pieces of broken basins, broken glass, and bits of shoe-latchets, although when they obtained them they esteemed them as if they had been the greatest of treasures. One of the seamen for a latchet received a piece of gold weighing two dollars and a half, and others, for other things of much less value, obtained more. Again, for new silver coin they would give everything they possessed, whether it was worth two or three doubloons or one or two balls of cotton. Even for pieces of broken pipe-tubes they would take them and give anything for them, until when I thought it wrong, I prevented it. And I made them presents of thousands of things which I had, that I might win their esteem and also that they might be made good Christians and be disposed to the service of your Majesties and the whole Spanish nation, and help us to obtain the things which we require and of which there is abundance in their country.

And these people appear to have neither religion nor idolatry, except that they believe that good and evil come from the skies; and they firmly believed that our ships and their crews, with myself, came from the skies, and with this persuasion, after having lost their fears, they always received us. And yet this does not proceed from ignorance, for they are very ingenious, and some of them navigate their seas in a wonderful manner and give good account of things, but because they never saw people dressed or ships like ours.

And as soon as I arrived in the Indies, at the first island at which I touched, I captured some of them, that we might learn from them and obtain intelligence of what there was in those parts. And as soon as we understood each other they were of great service to us; but yet, from frequent conversation which I had with them, they still believe we came from the skies. These were the first to express that idea, and others ran from house to house, and to the neighboring villages, crying out, "Come and see the people from the skies." And thus all of them, men and women, after satisfying themselves of their safety, came to us without reserve, great and small, bringing us some thing to eat and drink, and which they gave to us most affectionately.

They have many canoes in those islands propelled by oars, some of them large and others small, and many of them with eight or ten paddles of a side, not very wide, but all of one trunk, and a boat cannot keep way with them by oars, for they are incredibly fast; and with these they navigate all the islands, which are innumerable, and obtain their articles of traffic. I have seen some of these canoes with sixty or eighty men in them, and each with a paddle.

Among the islands I did not find much diversity of formation in the people, nor in their customs, nor their language. They all understand each other, which is remarkable; and I trust Your Highnesses will determine on their being converted to our faith, for which they are very well disposed.

I have already said that I went 107 leagues along the coast of Juana, from east to west, Thus, according to my track, it is larger than England and Scotland together, for, besides these 107 leagues, there were further west two provinces to which I did not go, one of which is called Cibau, the people of which are born with tails; which provinces must be about fifty or sixty leagues long, according to what I can make out from the Indians I have with me, who know all the islands. The other island, (Española) is larger in circuit than the whole of Spain, from the Straits of Gibralter (the Columns) to Fuentarabia in Biscay, as I sailed 138 long leagues in a direct line from west to east. Once known it must be desired, and once seen one desires never to leave it; and which, being taken possession of for their Highnesses, and the people being at present in a condition lower than I can possibly describe, the sovereigns of Castile may dispose of it in any manner they please in the most convenient places. In this Española, and in the best district, where are gold mines, and, on the other side, from thence to terra firma, as well as from thence to the Great Khan, where everything is on a splendid scale—I have taken possession of a large town, to which I gave the name of La Navidad, and have built a fort in it, in every respect complete. And I have left sufficient people in it to take care of it, with artillery and provisions for more than a year; also a boat and coxswain with the equipments, in complete friendship with the King of the islands, to that degree that he delighted to call me and look on me as his brother. And should they fall out with these people, neither he nor his subjects know anything of weapons, and go naked, as I have said, and they are the most timorous people in the world. The few people left there are sufficient to conquer the country, and the island would thus remain without danger to them, they keeping order among themselves.

In all these islands it appeared to me the men are contented with one wife, but to their governor or king they allow twenty. The women seem to work more than the men. I have not been able to discover whether they respect personal property, for it appeared to me things were common to all, especially in the particular of provisions. Hitherto I have not seen in any of these islands any monsters, as there were supposed to be; the people, on the contrary, are generally well formed, nor are they black like those of the Guinea, saving their hair and they do not reside in places exposed to the sun's rays. It is true that the sun is most powerful there, and it is only twenty-six degrees from the equator. In this last winter those islands which were mountainous were cold, but they were accustomed to it, with good food and plenty of spices and hot nutriment. Thus I have found no monsters nor heard of any, except at an island which is the second in going to the Indies, and which is inhabited by a people who are considered in all the islands as ferocious, and who devour human flesh. These people have many canoes, which scour all the islands of India, and plunder all they can. They are not worse formed than the others, but they wear the hair long like women, and use bows and arrows of the same kind of cane, pointed with a piece of hard wood instead of iron, of which they have none. They are fierce compared with the other people, who are in general but sad cowards; but I do not consider them in any other way superior to them. These are they who trade in women, who inhabit the first island met with in going from Spain to the Indies, in which there are no men whatever. They have no effeminate exercise, but bows and arrows, as before said, of cane, with which they arm themselves, and use shields of copper, of which they have plenty.

There is another island, I am told, larger than Española, the natives of which have no hair. In this there is gold without limit, and of this and the others I have Indians with me to witness.

In conclusion, referring only to what has been effected by this voyage, which was made with so much haste, Your Highnesses may see that I shall find as much gold as desired with the very little assistance afforded to me; there is as much spice and cotton as can be wished for, and also gum, which hitherto has only been found in Greece, in the island of Chios, and they may sell it as they please, and the mastich, as much as may be desired, and slaves, also, who will be idolators. And I believe that I have rhubarb, and cinnamon, and a thousand other things I shall find, which will be discovered by those whom I have left behind, for I did not stop at any cape when the wind enabled me to navigate, except at the town of Navidad, where I was very safe and well taken care of. And in truth much more I should have done if the ships had served me as might have been expected. This is certain, that the Eternal God our Lord gives all things to those who obey Him, and the victory when it seems impossible, and this, evidently, is an instance of it, for although people have talked of these lands, all was conjecture unless proved by seeing them, for the greater part listened and judged more by hearsay than by anything else.

Since, then, our Redeemer has given this victory to our illustrious King and Queen and celebrated their reigns by such a great thing, all Christendom should rejoice and make great festivals, and give solemn thanks to the Blessed Trinity, with solemn praises for the exaltation of so much people to our holy faith; and next for the temporal blessings which not only Spain but they will enjoy in becoming Christians, and which last may shortly be accomplished.

Written in the caravel off the Canary Islands, on the fifteenth of February, ninety-three.

The following is introduced into the letter after being closed:

"After writing the above, being in the Castilian Sea (off the coast of Castile), I experienced so severe a wind from south and southeast that I have been obliged to run today into this port of Lisbon, and only by a miracle got safely in, from whence I intended to write to Your Highnesses. In all parts of the Indies I have found the weather like that of May, where I went in ninety-three days, and returned in seventy-eight, saving these thirteen days of bad weather that I have been detained beating about in this sea. Every seaman here says that never was so severe a winter, nor such loss of ships.

XXXII.

THE WILL OF CHRISTOPHER COLUMBUS. CERTIFIED COPY IN THE COLLECTION OF THE DUKE OF VERAGUA, MADRID.

In the name of the Most Holy Trinity, who inspired me with the idea and afterward made it perfectly clear to me, that I could navigate and go to the Indies from Spain, by traversing the ocean westwardly; which I communicated to the King, Don Ferdinand, and to the Queen, Doña Isabella, our Sovereigns; and they were pleased to furnish me the necessary equipment of men and ships, and to make me their Admiral over the said ocean, in all parts lying to the west of an imaginary line drawn from pole to pole, a hundred leagues west of the Cape de Verde and Azore Islands, also appointing me their Viceroy and Governor over all continents and islands that I might discover beyond the said line westwardly; with the right of being succeeded in the said offices by my eldest son and his heirs forever, and a grant of the tenth part of all things found in the said jurisdiction; and of all rents and revenues arising from it; and the eighth of all the lands and everything else, together with the salary corresponding to my rank of Admiral, Viceroy and Governor, and all other emoluments accruing thereto, as is more fully expressed in the title and agreement sanctioned by their Highnesses.

And it pleased the Lord Almighty that in the year one thousand fourhundred and ninety-two, I should discover the continent of the Indies and many islands, among them Española, which the Indians call Ayte and the Menicongos, Cipango. I then returned to Castile to their Highnesses, who approved of my undertaking a second enterprise for further discoveries and settlements, and the Lord gave me victory over the Island of Española, which extends six hundred leagues, and I conquered it and made it tributary; and I discovered many islands inhabited by cannibals, and seven hundred to the west of Española, among which is Jamaica, which we call Santiago; and three hundred and thirty-three leagues of continent from south to west, besides a hundred and seven to the north, which I discovered on my first voyage; together with many islands, as may more clearly, be seen by my letters, memorials and maritime charts. And as we hope in God that before long a good and great revenue will be derived from the above islands and continent, of which, for the reason aforesaid, belong to me the tenth and the eighth, with the salaries and emoluments specified above; and considering that we are mortal, and that it is proper for every one to settle his affairs, and to leave declared to his heirs and successors the property he possesses or may have a right to: Wherefore, I have concluded to create an entailed estate (mayorazgo) out of the said eighth of the lands, places and revenues, in the manner which I now proceed to state:

In the first place I am to be succeeded by Don Diego, my son, who, in case of death without children, is to be succeeded by my other son, Ferdinand; and should God dispose of him also without leaving children and without my having any other son, then my brother, Don Bartholomew, is to succeed; and after him his eldest son; and if God should dispose of him without heirs, he shall be succeeded by his sons from one to another forever; or in the failure of a son, to be succeeded by Don Ferdinand, after the same manner, from son to son, successively; or in their place by my brothers, Bartholomew and Diego. And should it please the Lord that the estate, after having continued some time in the line of any of the above successors, should stand in need of an immediate and lawful-male heir, the succession shall then devolve to the nearest relation, being a man of legitimate birth and bearing the name of Columbus derived from his father and his ancestors. This entailed estate shall in nowise be inherited by a woman, except in case that no male is to be found, either in this or any other quarter of the world, of my real lineage, whose name as well as that of his ancestors, shall have always been Columbus. In such an event (which may God forefend), then the female of legitimate birth most nearly related to the preceding possessor of the estate shall succeed to it; and this is to be under the conditions herein stipulated at foot, which must be understood to extend as well to Don Diego, my son, as to the aforesaid and their heirs, every one of them, to be fulfilled by them; and failing to do so they are to be deprived of the succession for not having complied with what shall herein be expressed; and the estate to pass to the person most nearly related to the one who held the right; and the person thus succeeding shall in like manner forfeit the estate, should he also fail to comply with said conditions; and another person, the nearest of my lineage, shall succeed, provided he abide by them, so that they may be observed in the form prescribed. This forfeiture is not to be incurred for trifling matters, originating in lawsuits, but in important cases, when the glory of God, or my own, or that of my family may be concerned, which supposes a perfect fulfillment of all the things hereby ordained; all which I recommend to the Courts of Justice. And I supplicate His Holiness, who now is, and those who may succeed to the holy church, that if it should happen that this, my will and testament, has need of his holy order and command for its fulfillment, that such order be issued in virtue of obedience and under penalty of excommunication, and that it shall not be in any wise disfigured. And I also pray the King and Queen, our Sovereigns, and their eldest born, Prince Don Juan, our Lord and their successors, for the sake of the services I have done them, and because it is just, and that it may please them not to permit this, my will and constitution of my entailed estate to be any way altered, but to leave it in the form and manner which I have ordained forever, for the greater glory of the Almighty, and that it may be the root and basis of my lineage, and a memento of the services I have rendered their Highnesses; that, being born in Genoa, I came over to serve them in Castile and discovered to the west of terra firma the Indies and islands before mentioned. I accordingly pray their Highnesses to order that this, my privilege and testament, be held valid and be executed summarily, and without any opposition or demur, according to the letter. I also pray the grandees of the realm and the lords of the council, and all others having administration of justice to be pleased not to suffer this, my will and testament, to be of no avail, but to cause it to be fulfilled as by me ordained; it being just that a noble, who has served the King and Queen and the kingdom, should be respected in the disposition of his estate by will, testament, institution of entail or inheritance, and that the same be not infringed either in whole or in part.

In the first place, my son, Don Diego, and all my successors and descendents, as well as my brothers, Bartholomew and Diego, shall bear my arms, such as I shall leave them after my days, without inserting anything else in them; and they shall be their seal to seal with all. Don Diego, my son, or any other who may inherit this estate, on coming in possession of the inheritance, shall sign with the signature which I now make use of, which is an X with an S over it, and an M with a Roman A over it, and over that an S, and then a Greek Y, with an S over it, with its lines and points as is my custom, as may be seen by my signatures, of which there are many, and it will be seen by the present one.

He shall only write "The Admiral," whatever other titles the King may have conferred on him. This is to be understood as respects his signature, but not the enumeration of his titles, which he can make at full length if agreeable, only the signature is to be "The Admiral."

The said Don Diego, or any other inheritor of this estate, shall possess my offices of the Admiral of the Ocean, which is to the west of an imaginary line, which his Highness ordered to be drawn, running from pole to pole, a hundred leagues beyond the Azores, and as many more beyond the Cape de Verde Islands, over all of which I was made by their order, their Admiral of the Sea, with all the preeminences held by Don Henrique in the Admiralty of Castile; and they made me their Governor and Viceroy perpetually and forever, over all the islands and mainlands discovered, or to be discovered, for myself and heirs, as is more fully shown by my treaty and privileges as above mentioned.

Item. The said Don Diego, or any other inheritor of this estate, shall distribute the revenue which it may please our Lord to grant him, in the following manner, under the above penalty.

First. Of the whole income of this estate, now and at all times, and of whatever may be had or collected from it, he shall give the fourth part of it to my brother, Don Bartholomew Columbus, Adelantado of the Indies, and this is to continue until he shall have acquired an income of a million maravedis* for his support, and for the services he has rendered and will continue to render to this entailed estate; which million he is to receive, as stated, every year, if the said fourth amount to so much, and that he have nothing else: but if he possess a part or the whole of that amount in rents, that henceforth he shall not enjoy the said million, nor any part of it, except that he shall have in the fourth year part unto the said quantity of a million, if it should amount to so much; and as much as he shall have a revenue besides this fourth part, whatever sum of maravedis of known rent from property or perpetual offices, the said quantity of rent or revenue from property or offices shall be discontinued; and from said million shall be reserved whatever marriage portion he may receive with any female he may acquire or may have over and above his wife's dowry; and when it shall please God that he or his heirs and descendants shall derive from their property and offices a revenue of a million arising from rents, neither he nor his heirs shall enjoy any longer anything from the said fourth part of the entailed estate which shall remain with Don Diego, or whoever may inherit.

Item. From the revenues of the said estate, or from any fourth part of it (should its amount be adequate to it), shall be paid every year to my son Ferdinand two millions, till such time as his revenue shall amount to two millions, in the same form and manner as in the case of Bartholomew, who, as well as his heirs, are to have the million or the part that may be wanting.

Item. The said Don Diego or Don Bartholomew shall make out of the said estate, for my brother Diego, such provision as may enable him to live decently, as he is my brother, to whom I assign no particular sum, as he has attached himself to the church, and that will be given him which is right; and this is to be given him in a mass, and before anything shall have been received by Ferdinand, my son, or Bartholomew, my brother, or their heirs; and also according to the amount of the income of the estate. And in case of discord, the case is to be referred to two of our relations, or other men of honor; and should they disagree among themselves, they will choose a third person as arbitrator, being virtuous and not distrusted by either party.

Item. All this revenue which I bequeath to Bartholomew, to Ferdinand, and to Diego, shall be delivered to and received by them as prescribed under the obligation of being faithful and loyal to Diego, my son, or his heirs, they as well as their children; and should it appear that they, or any of them, had proceeded against him in anything touching his honor, or the prosperity of the family or of the estate either in word or deed, whereby might come a scandal and debasement to my family, and a detriment to my estate in that case, nothing further shall be given to them or his from that time forward, inasmuch as they are always to be faithful to Diego and his successors.

Item. As it was my intention, when I first instituted this entailed estate, to dispose, or that my son Diego should dispose for me,

*Approximately thirty-five hundred dollars.

of the tenth part of the income in favor of necessitous persons, as a tithe, and in commemoration of the Almighty, and Eternal God; and persisting still in this opinion, and hoping that his High Majesty will assist me, and those who may inherit it, in this or the New World, I have resolved that the said tithe shall be paid in the manner following:

First. It is to be understood that the fourth part of the revenue of the estate which I have ordained and directed to be given to Don Bartholomew, until he have an income of one million, includes the tenth of the whole revenue of the estate; and that, as in proportion as the income of my brother Don Bartholomew shall increase, as it has to be discounted from the revenue of the fourth part of entailed estate, that the said revenue shall be calculated, to know how much the tenth part amounts to; and the part which exceeds what is necessary to make up the million for Don Bartholomew shall be received by each of my family as may most stand in need of it, discounting it from the said tenth, if their income do not amount to the fifty thousand maravedis; and should any of these come to have an income to this amount, such a part shall be awarded to them as two persons, chosen for the purpose, may determine along with Don Diego or his heirs. Thus, it is to be understood that the million which I leave to Bartholomew comprehends the tenth of the whole revenue of the estate; which revenue is to be distributed among my nearest and most needy relations in the manner I have directed; and when Don Bartholomew has an income of one million, and that nothing more shall be due to him on account of said fourth part, then Don Diego, my son, or the persons which I shall herein point out, shall inspect the accounts and so direct that the tenth of the revenue shall still continue to be paid to the most necessitous members of my family that may be found in this or any other quarter of the world, who shall diligently be sought out; and they are to be paid out of the fourth part from which Don Bartholomew is to derive his million, which sums are to be taken into account, and deducted from the said tenth, which, should it amount to more, the overplus, as it arises from the fourth part, shall be given to the most necessitous persons as aforesaid; and should it not be sufficient, that Don Bartholomew shall have it until his own estate goes on increasing, leaving the said million in part or in the whole.

Item. The said Don Diego, my son, or whoever may be the inheritor, shall appoint two persons of conscience and authority, and most nearly related to the family who are to examine the revenue and its amount carefully, and to cause the tenth to be paid out of the fourth from which Don Bartholomew is to receive his million to his most necessitous members of my family who may be found here or elsewhere, whom they shall look for diligently upon their consciences; and as it might happen that said Don Diego or others after him, for reasons which may concern their own welfare, or the credit support of the estate, may be unwilling to make known the full amount of the income, nevertheless I charge him on his conscience to pay the sum aforesaid and charge them on their souls and consciences not to denounce or make it known, except with the consent of Don Diego, or the person that may succeed him, but let the above tithe be paid in the manner I have directed.

Item. In order to avoid all disputes in the choice of the two nearest relations who are to act with Don Diego or his heirs, I hereby elect Don Bartholomew, my brother, for one, and Don Fernando, my son, for the other; and when these two shall enter upon the business they shall choose two other persons among the most trusty, and most nearly related, and these again shall elect two others, when it shall be question of commencing the examination; and thus it shall be managed with diligence from one to the other, as well in this as in the other of government, for the service and glory of God, and the benefit of the said entailed estate.

Item. I also enjoin Diego, or any one that may inherit the estate, to have and maintain in the city of Genoa one person of our lineage to reside there with his wife, and appoint him a sufficient revenue to enable him to live decently, as a person closely connected with the family, of which he is to be the root and basis in that city; from which great good may accrue to him, inasmuch as I was born there, and came from thence.

Item. The said Don Diego, or whoever shall inherit the estate, must remit in bills, or in any other way, all such sums as he may be able to save out of the revenue of the estate, and direct purchases to be made in his name, or that of his heirs, in a fund in the Bank of St. George,* which gives an interest of six per cent. and is secure money; and this shall be devoted to the purpose I am about to explain.

Item. As it becomes every man of rank and property to serve God, either personally or by means of his wealth, and as all moneys deposited with St. George are quite safe, and Genoa is a noble city and powerful by the sea, and as at the same time that I undertook to set out upon that discovery of the Indies, it was with the intention of supplicating the King and Queen, our lords, that whatever moneys should be derived from the said Indies should be invested in the conquest of Jerusalem; and as I did so supplicate them, if they do this, it will be well; if not, at all events the said Diego, or such persons as may succeed him in this trust, to collect together all the money he can, and accompany the King, our lord, should he go to the conquest of Jerusalem, or else go there himself with all the force he can command; and in pursuing this intention, it will please the Lord to assist toward the accomplishment of the plan; and should he not be able to effect the conquest of the whole, no doubt he will achieve in part. Let him therefore collect and make a fund of all his wealth in St. George in Genoa, and let it multiply there until such time as it may appear to him that something of consequence may be effected as respects the project on Jerusalem; for I believe that when their Highnesses shall see that this is contemplated, they will wish to realize it themselves, or will afford him, as their servant and vassal, the means of doing it for them.

*The great financial corporation of Genoa.

Item. I charge my son Diego and my descendants, especially whoever may inherit this estate, which consists, as aforesaid, of the tenth of whatsoever may be had or found in the Indies, and the eighth part of the lands and rents, all which, together with my rights and emoluments as admiral, viceroy and governor, amount to more than twenty-five per cent., I say, that I require of him to employ all this revenue, as well as his person, and all the means in his power, in well and faithfully serving and supporting their Highnesses, or their successors, even to the loss of life and property; since it was their Highnesses, next to God, who first gave the means of getting and achieving this property, although, it is true, I came over these realms to invite them to the enterprise, and that a long time elapsed before any provision was made for carrying it into eexcution; which, however, is not surprising, as this was an undertaking of which all the world was ignorant, and no one had any faith in it; wherefore, I am by so much more indebted to them, as well as because they have since also much favored and promoted me.

Item. I also require of Diego, or whosoever may be in possession of the estate, that in the case of any schism taking place in the church of God, or that any person of whatever class or condition should attempt to despoil it of its property and honors they hasten to offer at the feet of his Holiness, that is, if they are not heretics (which God forbid), their persons, power and wealth, for the purpose of suppressing such schism, and preventing any spoliation of the honor and property of the church.

Item. I command the said Diego, or whoever may possess the said estate, to labor and strive for the honor, welfare and aggrandisement of the city of Genoa, and to make use of all his power and means in defending and enhancing the good and credit of that republic, in all things not contrary to the service of the church of God, or the high dignity of the King and Queen, our lords and their successors.

Item. The said Diego, or whoever may possess or succeed to the estate, out of the fourth part of the whole revenue, from which, as aforesaid, is to be taken a tenth, when Don Bartholomew or his heirs shall have saved the two millions, or part of them, and when the time shall come for making a distribution among our relations, shall apply and invest the said tenth in providing marriages for such daughters of our lineage as may require it, and in doing all the good in their power.

Item. When a suitable time shall arrive, he shall order a church to be built in the island of Española, and in the most convenient spot, to be called Santa Maria de la Conception; to which is to be annexed an hospital, upon the best possible plan, like those of Italy and Castile, and a chapel is to be erected in which to say mass for the good of my soul, and those of my ancestors and successors with great devotion, since no doubt it will please the Lord to give us a sufficient revenue for this and the afore-mentioned purposes.

Item. I also order Diego my son, or whosoever may inherit after him, to spare no pains in having and maintaining in the island of

Espanola, four good professors in theology, to the end and aim of their studying and laboring to convert to our holy faith the inhabitants of the Indies; and in proportion as by God's will the revenue of the estate shall increase in the same degree shall the number of teachers and devout persons increase, who are to strive to make Christians of the natives; in attaining which no expense should be thought too great. And in commemoration of all that I hereby ordain, and of the foregoing, a monument of marble shall be erected in the said church of La Conception, in the most conspicuous place, to serve as a record of what I here enjoin on the said Diego, as well as to other persons who may look upon it; which marble shall contain an inscription to the same effect.

Item. I also require of Diego, my son, and whosoever may succeed him in the estate, that every time, and as often as he confesses, he first show his obligation, or a copy of it, to the confessor, praying him to read it through, that he may be enabled to inquire respecting its fulfillment; from which will redound great good and happiness to his soul.

S.
S. A. S.
X. M. Y.
El Almirante.

www.ingramcontent.com/pod-product-compliance
Lightning Source LLC
Chambersburg PA
CBHW031409160426
43196CB00007B/958